THE COMPLETE AKITA

American, Canadian, Mexican, International (C.A.C.I.B.) Champion Gin-Gin Haiyaku-Go of Sakusaku, a brindle male born August 7, 1970. His show record of 225-plus Bests of Breed and over 50 group placements set an early record for the breed. "Chester" won the Akita 1977 Specialty and held an R.O.M. title in the breed. Among his awards was the title of top winning Akita in 1973, 1976 and 1977. He was the first Best in Show Akita in Canada.

Ludwig

DEDICATED

—*to our daughters, Shelley Funk Neuss, Susan Linderman Sanett and Tracy Linderman Salce, our deepest gratitude for their inspiration and help in putting this manuscript together.*

—*to our husbands, Jerry Linderman and Marty Funk, the biggest "Thank You" of all. Without your devotion to us, this book could never have been written.*

THE

COMPLETE

AKITA

by Joan M. Linderman

and Virginia Funk

1985 — Third Printing
HOWELL BOOK HOUSE INC.
230 Park Avenue, New York, N.Y. 10169

Library of Congress Cataloging in Publication Data

Linderman, Joan M.
   The complete Akita

   Bibliography: p. 215
   1. Akita dogs.   I. Funk, Virginia.   II. Title
III. Title: Akita
SF429.A65L56   1983   636.7′3   83-6180
ISBN 0-87605-006-2

Contents

About the Authors

THE COMPLETE AKITA owes its authenticity to two people whose combined knowledge makes this the definitive work on the breed in the United States.

JOAN M. LINDERMAN has owned, shown and bred some of the top Akitas in the U.S.A. for twenty years, including the first American, Mexican and Canadian international champion of the breed. Her kennel name, Sakusaku, appears on five of the Akita breed's top producers, winners of the coveted Register of Merit award of the Akita Club of America.

Mrs. Linderman has served the ACA as president. She was a member and director of the American Akita Breeders, Inc.

A contributing member of *The Akita Review,* a quarterly magazine, she was co-author of the *Breeding and Whelping Manual,* published by the ACA, and a contributor to the breed manual, *The Akita: A Guide.* She was a co-editor of *The Akita News.*

Mrs. Linderman has judged Akitas at numerous all-Akita match and specialty shows. She was the 1978 recipient of the Gaines Medal for Good Sportsmanship.

With her husband Jerry, Mrs. Linderman has traveled extensively in Japan and the United States tracking down information on the Akita breed. This has resulted in the most extensive collection of breed documentation in America today.

VIRGINIA FUNK is an award-winning professional writer and a breeder-exhibitor and AKC-approved judge of German Shepherds. She is also approved to judge Belgian Sheepdogs and Belgian Tervurens.

Her dog column, *Leash & Collar,* published in the Tri-Valley *Herald and News* in California, won the "Best All-round Writing Job" Award in 1970 from the Dog Writers Association of America. Eleven years later, the DWAA again presented her with the top award in Best Columns and News Reports for newspapers under 150,000 circulation. She has also written articles for *Dog Fancy, Popular Dogs, People on Parade* and other magazines. For ten years she has been a regular contributor to the AARP publication *Modern Maturity.* In the mid '70s she was full-time writer and secretary for Mitsui Fudosan (USA) Inc., a subsidiary of Mitsui & Co., Japan, one of the world's largest trading companies.

She is a member of the Board of Directors of International Guiding Eyes, Inc., for which she was founder of its annual benefit match show and show chairman three times.

Biographical data for DONALD W. LUSK, who contributes the excellent first chapter, *The Development of the Akita in Japan,* are given in that chapter.

Joan M. Linderman   Virginia Funk

Acknowledgments

For the chapter on the Akita in Japan, a special acknowledgment to Donald Lusk, student of the breed.

To Vera Bohac and Cheryl Langan, for their contribution of the breed history and pictures of early and present dogs in Canada.

To Donald Brust, D.V.M. for information included in Chapters 9 and 10.

To Dr. Shinichi Ishiguro, Dr. Ogasawara, Richard Kawamoto, Sadako Cunningham and Walter Imai, just a few of the devoted lovers of the Akita breed and friends, who have contributed pictures and background history of the breed from their files.

To Gerald N. Linderman, Eric F. Linderman and Warren Linderman for illustrations.

To Margaret Bryant, devotee of the breed, close friend and fellow author, for her assistance and support.

To all the people who have supplied photos and information but are too many to list individually, a gracious "Thank You." Most of your names and/or pictures appear elsewhere in the text.

And last, but not least, our appreciation to the Akita Club of Tampa Bay (Florida) for compiling the list of R.O.M. Dogs and Bitches for this book.

Foreword

WELCOME TO MY DREAM

For many years, the dearly beloved animal that has had its place in my household has been the exotic Japanese breed of dog called the Akita.

In 1964 I purchased my first Akita, a bitch, and watched her grow from a twelve-weeks-old furry bundle of frolicsome love into an alert, responsive adult dog, family member, and guardian. Mitsubachi, "Honey Bee," passed out of our lives after eleven years of devoted companionship. My family and I have bred, raised, shown, trained and loved many others since Honey Bee came into our lives. In the process, I became a student of the breed.

Living in the United States, I had become accustomed to thinking of the Akita as a breed that still had a long way to go before becoming well-standardized and truly sound. Naturally, I wanted to do my part to hasten that day. In an effort to find a superior animal with which to improve my breeding program, I travelled to Japan and attended Akita shows throughout that country.

There are no words to describe the breathtaking sight that met my eyes at these shows: up to 500 Akitas, all alike in type, glorious in color, and sound in body. It was here that my dream was born, and with it this book.

I dare to dream that one day the Akita in this country will have developed into as beautiful, majestic, and sound an animal as the breed now is in Japan. I dare to dream that one day every Akita fancier in the United States will know the thrill of pleasure and admiration that I still feel on viewing the awesome Akitas of Japan.

For the person who truly loves the Akita breed, there is nothing more inspiring than to produce a litter of puppies that is superior to the animals you have had before. I have had that feeling, so I know.

This book contains everything you need to know to play your part, not merely in propagating the Akita breed, but in improving it. Dare to dream with me, and together we will create something that will excite the admiration of dog lovers throughout the world.

—Joan M. Linderman

1

The Development
of the Akita in Japan

by DONALD W. LUSK

WHEN JOAN ASKED ME to write an introductory chapter for this book, I had no idea what a difficult task it would be to attempt to capsule a history of the origins of the Akita from antiquity to the period immediately following the Second World War.

The first obstacle one encounters is the limited research and written material available; secondly, the inevitable difficulty in securing accurate translations of such material from the original Japanese; thirdly, there is diversity of opinion even among the handful of scholars who have made a serious effort to search out and chronicle the facts.

Though Japan offers us over 2,600 years of recorded history and civilization, the fragments of that long and colorful history which shed any conclusive light on the true origins of the Akita dog, as we know it today, are sparse indeed.

There are but a handful of Japanese scientific and lay authors who over the past century have devoted significant effort to sorting out the origins and development of the Japanese type dog in general, and the Akita in particular. Their conclusions and speculations are based on archeological, zoological, anthropological, and ethnological viewpoints. Also important are those whose studies have been primarily pursued through review of what written history has been documented by folklore and those closely identified with "Japanese dog culture."

One of the most disciplined investigations of the origin of the Akita is currently being conducted by J. Hooper and N. Rhoden of Oakland, California. Theirs is the only research of which I am aware which is based on the pure biological aspects of the Akita. Their findings, when published, may prove to be highly surprising, and certainly more scientifically conclusive than most.

Some of the more accepted and respected authorities on the subject in Japan include: Dr. Toku Uchida, author of *Inu No Hon* (Book on Dogs); Dr. Shosaburo Watase; Mr. Hirokichi Saito, founder of Nihon-Ken, and author of *Nihon No Inu To Okami* (Dogs and Wolves of Japan); Dr. Noburo Sagara of Waseda University; Dr. Tei Uchida; Mr. Hiroyoshe Saito; and Mr. Naoto Kajiwara, author of *My Thoughts On The Akita Dog*.

It was long believed that people first migrated to the Japanese Islands around 4,000 years ago, bringing with them the *Jamon* culture of hunters. However, more recent archeological finds indicate that Japanese history dates farther back into the Stone Age. A study of reconstructed skeletal remains and fossils from the Jamon Period indicate that domesticated dogs first appeared during this time, and were used for hunting and protection. Though it is not known whether these dogs had stand-up ears and curled tails, or if they were originally from Japan, it may be assumed that they were related to the present Akita dog.

The Bronze Age of Yayoi followed the Stone Age. Drawings and artifacts of this period picture dogs with stand-up ears and half curled tails, and other distinct features of the Japanese type dog. During the reign of Emperor Jinmu (660 B.C.) new dogs were brought from China and Korea.

From this point in history forward, there are many and conflicting theories. However, it is generally accepted that the traditional Japanese type dogs evolved into their various distinctive forms, greatly influenced by their habitat and geographical location. In areas where there were rapid civilization and exposure to outside influences, the purity of the breed tended to disappear due to much cross-breeding. In general, the Japanese dogs which were declared as natural monuments came from the remote mountain areas where civilization was slow to make its inroads, and where the purity of the dog breeds was maintained.

There are seven breeds of Japanese dogs that were declared as natural monuments, and named according to their place of origin. They were also classified by sizes into the large, medium and small dogs. The large dog is the Akita, from the Odate area. There is no other known large Japanese dog surviving today.

The name Akita-Inu (Akita Dog) was not used until September 1931, at which time the Akita was designated as a natural monument. Prior to that time, dogs from the Odate Region were called the "Odate Dogs." During the Feudal Period these dogs were called the "Nambu-Inu" (Southern Regional Dog). Those dogs which were used for fighting purposes were called either "Kuriya-Inu" while those used for hunting by the mountain villagers were called "Matagi-Inu." The word Matagi refers to hunter.

Thus, since ancient times, Japanese dogs were named according to their locale, or their roles as domesticated animals.

It seems clear that the direct forebears of the Akita as we know it today were native to Akita Prefecture, the northernmost province on the main Japanese Island of Honshu. The historical epicenter of the present day Akita is the City of Odate in Akita Prefecture.

There have been several organizations evolved in Japan which have contributed significantly to the preservation and restoration of the Akita.

During the Dog Fighting Era of the Meiji Period (1868-1912), there was a dog fighting club called Enyukai. The Aiken Kyokai was another dog fighting club formed during the Taisho Period (1912-1925).

Akitainu Hozonkai, the largest and most dominant Akita Club in Japan today, was established in 1927. A branch of the organization was founded in Los Angeles during 1969.

Nipponken Hozonkai (Nippo) was established in 1928, and Akitainu Kyokai (Akikyo) was established in 1948.

Each of the three forementioned organizations has developed an Akita Breed Standard, and maintains an Akita Registry.

One of the most significant events in the restoration and preservation of the Akita was the tremendous attention commanded throughout Japan and the entire world by the moving story of an Akita dog named Hachi-Ko. No dog before or since has so touched the hearts of people everywhere.

In November, 1923, a puppy was born in Akita Prefecture which showed great promise of being of true Akita type. At the age of two months it was sent to Professor Eizaburo Ueno in Tokyo, who had long coveted a fine Akita dog. The Professor named the puppy Hachi, and called him Hachi-Ko. At that time, Professor Ueno's residence was in a suburb of Tokyo in the vicinity of Shibuya Station, and he commuted by train from that station to the agricultural experimental station at Nishikebara where he worked. Hachi-Ko accompanied his master in the morning and in the evening as he went to and from work. On May 21, 1925, when Hachi-Ko was one and one-half years old, he was at Shibuya Station as usual, waiting for his master's arrival on the four o'clock train. Professor Ueno would in fact never arrive, as he had been struck down by a fatal stroke at the University that day. Hachi-Ko was cared for by relatives and friends of the family, but he continued to go to Shibuya Station each day to await his master's arrival. Hachi-Ko's vigil continued until March 8, 1934, when at the age of 11 years and 4 months he died, still waiting in vain for the return of his beloved master.

Fiction could not have given birth to such a sentimental story of fidelity, courage, and a dog's love of man. Response throughout Japan, and indeed the whole world, was spontaneous, as eulogies and warm words of condolence poured into Japan from young and old, rich and poor.

Today, commuters through Shibuya Station in Tokyo still must pass the imposing statue of Hachi-Ko, erected in loving memory to the venerable dog. His proud figure, sculptured in bronze and set high on a granite block, stands as a mute evidence of the place in Japan's cultural and social history occupied by the Akita dog.

No story of the Akita would be complete without mention of the rather extraordinary circumstances surrounding the first Akita to come to America. Years before the Akita caught the eye and the fancy of American military occupation personnel in Japan following World War II, a famous American woman discovered and learned to love the unique character and qualities of this magnificent breed. What must have enraptured her most were the spiritual rather than the physical characteristics of the Akita, for she had been blind since birth.

Helen Keller, world-famed scholar, lecturer, author, educator, humanitarian, first visited the Orient and Japan in 1937, where she commenced a grueling ten week speaking tour, visiting thirty-nine cities, and giving ninety-nine lectures to more than a million people. Her tour would take her eventually to Akita City, a town of about sixty thousand residents at that time. During an interview with reporters earlier, she had indicated that she would like to have an Akita dog. The notion probably came to her while in Tokyo where she had learned of the Akita dog Hachi-Ko, and was touched by his story. At Akita City, Mr. Ichiro Ogasawara, a member of the Akita Police Department, presented Miss Keller with one of his own new puppies, Kamikaze-Go. It should be remembered that purebred Akitas were at that time virtually non-existent outside of Akita Prefecture, and very scarce even there.

Kamikaze-Go returned to the United States with Helen Keller aboard the liner Chichibu Maru. "Kami," as he was affectionately called, went to live with Helen Keller at her estate in a suburb of New York. Unfortunately, Kami became ill and died in November of the same year at the tender age of eight months.

In June, 1939, a second Akita, Kenzan-Go, was sent to Miss Keller from her admirers in Japan. Kenzan-Go lived with Miss Keller until his death around 1944 or 1945.

So started the strange introduction of the Akita to America, and the ensuing interest in this exotic breed from Japan which finally culminated in recognition of the Akita in America by the American Kennel Club in 1973.

Three events which in combination contributed significantly to focusing attention on the Akita dog during the two decades preceding World War II were: the saga of Hachi-Ko, the tour of Japan by Helen Keller and her involvement with the breed, and the declaration of the Akita as a natural monument. Had these events not occurred, one must wonder if the Akita, as a distinctive and identifiable breed, would have survived.

After the Akita was declared a natural monument, there is ample recorded evidence of a strong surge of activity, in the Odate area in particular, to restore the Japanese Akita dog to its original state. It is fortunate indeed that the road back for the Akita started in the 1920's, for had it not, World War II, which further decimated the ranks of the breed, would probably have seen the final extinction of the Akita dog.

That the Akita did survive the Second World War is in itself a miracle, for that great conflict took its toll of dogs as well as people. The ravages of war caused the normal shortages of commodities, and the shortage of food rapidly became serious. The Akita dog, which consumed the most food among Japanese dogs, suffered greatly, and gradually dwindled in numbers. Dog and cat pelts began to be used to provide cold weather clothing for the military. The large Akita dog thus became a primary target to be captured for such uses. According to dog owners who lived in Akita Prefecture at that time, the Police Department issued orders for dog catchers to go into all of the towns and villages to capture and kill all dogs, except for the Shepherd, which was being used as a military dog. It is said that a considerable number of Akita dogs were captured and clubbed to death. During these dark days of

1941-1945, the Akita was threatened with virtual extinction.

No one knows for sure how many Akita dogs survived the Second World War. One record of post war dogs is found in the *Akitainu Tokuhon* (Akita Dog Textbook) by Mr. Kiyono. It lists several dogs of the Ichinoseki line, including Ichinoseki-Go, Shintora-Go, Hachiman-Go, Tatenohana-Go, Arawashi-Go and Dainimatsumine-Go. The Dewa line consisted of Raiden-yo, Dewawaka-Go, Taishu-Go, Tatemitsu-Go, and Shinmutsu-Go.

According to the Akiho magazine, some of the dogs shown at the 12th Akiho Show in April, 1948, were from the wartime period. They include Bushi-Go, Tamazakura-Go, Habubotan-Go, Furuhime-Go, Tomoe-Go, and Mitzukaze-Go, all of which were considered as Tokuyu (superior) dogs. There were about 60 Akita entries at this show.

During the period 1948-1950, many historically famous Akita dogs were produced; including Goromaro-Go (regarded as the most important foundation stud dog in the restoration process), Jiroraru-Go (littermate to Goromaru-Go), Torafusa-Go, Long-Go, Dainikisaragi-Go, Shinzan-Go, Shinko-Go, Tohuko-Go, Arawai-Go, Tsukasa-Go, Kurogani-Go, Homon-Go, Tatenoryu-Go, Tamagumo-Go, Sachinishiki-Go, Kincho-Go, Shinben-Go, and Tanihibiki-Go.

As the Akita dog became more popular and increased in numbers, the lineage of the dogs became a matter of great emphasis among the serious breeders. During this period emerged the two main lines (the Ichinoseki and the Dewa) which became the starting point for the Akita breed as it gained its first foothold in America during the 1950's and 1960's.

This is where the story of the Akita in America begins.

DON LUSK, President of the Akita Club of America in 1980-81, started breeding and exhibiting Akitas in 1970. His kennel affix is Arashi Hoshi Akitas.

18

Don served the Akita Club as a Director, Chairman of the Code of Ethics Committee and Trial Board Committee, and Member of its Standard Review Committee.

He was Founder/President of the Akita Club of Greater Los Angeles and Past President of Akitainu-Hozonkai, Los Angeles Branch, which is the Japanese Society for Preservation of the Akita Dog. He is a member of the Akita Club of Puget Sound and of the Dog Writers Association of America.

The Co-Publisher/Editor of *The Akita Journal,* his articles on the breed have been published in America, Canada and Japan. He has presented slides and lectures on the Akita in Portland, Los Angeles, San Francisco, Houston, Chicago, New York, Seattle and Canada. He served as ring steward at the Akita National Specialties held in Chicago (1978) and in Houston (1979). He has judged Akita match shows in California, Arizona and Texas.

Two Akita males in a typical face-off position (Terrier style) is the way they have always been shown in Japan.

2

The Early Basic Strains

Great Dogs of Japan and Their Influence on the Breed

Pedigree Studies

Extensive research has been done on the Akita family tree. However, for the period prior to 1930 few records and pictures are available.

In tracing early pedigrees, two dogs, Tochini-Go and Babagoma-Go, frequently appear. They are said to be responsible for the present main Akita line in Japan.

Tochini-Go, a male popularly called "Aka," was owned by Mr. Isumi, the first chairman of Akiho. Aka was sired by a white Akita fighting dog called Mitane-Go. His dam, Norogomame-Go, was colored red goma. (When two words describe a coat color, the first word is the primary color and the second refers to the color of the undercoat. "Red goma" is a red outer coat with a gray under coat.) An early photo reveals one flopped ear and a coiled tail. Despite the ear fault, he impresses one as being a pure Japanese dog.

Babagoma-Go was a red female owned by the famous Mr. Kunio Ichinoseki, founder of the line which bears his name. Many famous old time Akitas stem from the Ichinoseki line which still flows through the blood of today's Akita dogs.

Our prime concern is Ichinoseki Goma-Go, call name Tsubaki Goma. An aka goma colored male, he stood 27.5

ICHINOSEKI TORA-GO, whelped Sept. 29, 1932
(red brindle/left ear down)

Kin-Go (pale red)	Tochini-Go (black brindle left ear down)	Mitane-Go	unknown / unknown
		Norogomame-Go	unknown / unknown
	Shiro-Go	Nidaioshinaiyama	Tateisami-Go / Goma-Go
		Aka-Go	Hamakaze-Go / Aka-Go
Tama-Go (red)	Tochini-Go	Mitane-Go	unknown / unknown
		Norogomame-Go	unknown / unknown
	Babagoma-Go (red tip)	Goma-Go	Goma-Go / Aka-Go
		Aka-Go	Hamakaze-Go / Aka-Go

ICHINOSEKI GOMA-GO, whelped April 10, 1943

Jugoro-Go	Saburo-Go	Ichinoseki Tora-Go	Kin-Go / Tama-Go
		Oshinai-Go	Tochisan-Go / Babagoma-Go
	Yama-Go	Ichinoseki Tora-Go	Kin-Go / Tama-Go
		Kuma-Go	Tora-Go / Aka-Go
Toshi-Go	Goma-Go	Ichinoseki Tora-Go	Kin-Go / Tama-Go
		Oshinai-Go	Tochisan-Go / Babagoma-Go
	Yama-Go	Ichinoseki Tora-Go	Kin-Go / Tama-Go
		Kuma-Go	Tora-Go / Aka-Go

inches tall. He was an imposing animal despite his weak rear and looseness of body. When bred to Futatsui Goma-Go (Matagi line), they produced the famous Goromaru-Go, regarded by many as the most important dog in the effort to bring the breed up to the Akita Standard after the ravages of World War II.

Goromaru and his three littermates were born January 8, 1948. Mr. Susumu Funakoshi bought Goromaru and recalls he was a precocious red and white pinto puppy with a large head, longer than average coat and rather small, deep set triangular shaped eyes. Goromaru and his brother, the 25″ Jiromaru-Go, were popular in the show ring.

The excellent quality of Goromaru offspring down through the years brought fame to this dog. When bred to the Ohira line of Akitas, e.g. Chimpei-Go and Shiromaru-Go, the results were spectacular, despite warnings from breeders who claimed the country-bred pinto would reproduce his color, not in favor at that time, and throw long coats known as "Moku."

Goromaru was bred to Chimpei-Go in 1950 and produced Kirjohime-Go, a lovely red bitch with white mask from Southern Akita Prefecture. She in turn was bred to the brindle dog, Tamagumo-Go and produced the bitch Kiyome-Go who, when bred to Daiun, whelped the incomparable bitch, Daiunme-Go. Daiunme had a luxurious black brindle coat and excellent frame. She produced three Meiyosho winners (those dogs who receive the highest award in Japan) in Bankomaru-Go, Kumohibiki-Go and Tamagumome-Go.

Bankomaru's littermate, Nanun-Go, produced the dog Kumomaru-Go, who in turn produced the beautiful red bitch, Meiyosho winner Tamayu-Go.

Another important Akita is Tamagumo-Go, an imposing brindle male sired by Arawashi-Go (Ichinoseki line) and whelped by Sansho-Go (Dewa line). Although he had quite a few small faults his markings, coat and masculinity could not be surpassed. The breadth and depth of his chest was to be admired. This worthy male can be found behind many of today's excellent Japanese Akitas.

22

The Dewa line existed at the same time as the Ichinoseki line. It derived its name from the black tip male Dewa-Go who was born February 1, 1941. It is said the ancestral dog behind him was Tachi-Go aka "Yari."

According to the late Mr. Naoei Sato, as quoted in *The Akita-inu,* "The Akita dogs of the Dewa line were noted for their large stately build and gentle temperament as household dogs, and yet were firm in their stand when necessary. However, the Dewa line soon began to lose its value as a representative of the Akita dog breed with the appearance of looseness of skin under the throat, loose baggy lips and other features which led to a departure from the Japanese dog image."

Immediately following World War II, Dewa-Go's great-grandson Kongo-Go began a show and breeding career which was said to have dominated the dog scene. The Dewa line went from Dewa-Go to Dewawaka-Go to Taishu-Go to Kongo-Go to Kincho-Go.

The kurogoma color, black sesame, dominated the Dewa line and was genetically very powerful. It held for generations. According to one source, Kongo's owner, Mr. Hashimoto, went so far as to label Kongo's picture with the words, "Kongo-Go, the National Treasure."

Although high awards were given Kongo and Kincho during the time breeders were trying to restore the Akita dog to what it had been in the past, the Dewa line declined by degrees. One would be hard-pressed to find its phenotype in Japan today.

GOROMARU-GO, whelped February 8, 1948
Owner, Mr. Susumu Funakoshi

Ichinoseki-Go	Jugoro-Go	Saburo-Go	Tora-Go
			Oshinai-Go
		Yama-Go	Tora-Go
			Kuma-Go
	Toshi-Go	Goma-Go	Tora-Go
			Oshinai-Go
		Yama-Go	Tora-Go
			Kuma-Go
Futatsui Goma-Go	Ichinoseki Aka-Go	Ichinoseki Toro-Go	Kin-Go
			Tama-Go
		Numatate Tora-Go	(unknown)
			(unknown)
	Shirayuki-Go	Osawaka-Go	(unknown)
			(unknown)
		Aniaka-Go	(unknown)
			(unknown)

24

Mrs. Funakoshi and the revered pelt of
Goromaru-Go. Japan, 1970.

25

ORYU-GO, whelped in 1953

		Jugoro-Go	Saburo-Go
	Ichinoseki Goma-Go		Yama-Go
		Toshi-Go	Goma-Go
Goromaru-Go			Yama-Go
		Ichinoseki-Go	Ichinoseki Tora-Go
	Futatsui Goma-Go		Numatate Tora-Go
		Shirayuki-Go	Osawaaka-Go
			Aniaka-Go
		Shiranami-Go	Kurowashi-Go
	Dainishirana-Go		Hachi-Go
		Akashime-Go	Suihoku-Go
Akashihime-Go			Yamime-Go
		Suihoku-Go	Heiku-Go
	Akahime-Go		Yamime-Go
		Yamime-Go	Muchi-Go
			Heitsume-Go

The famous Muchi-Go.

Azumazakura-Go.
Outstanding stud in
immediate back-
ground of a few early
imports.

27

Tamugumo-Go, whelped December 13, 1950 was a Meiyosho winner owned by Riyosuke Tadamoto.

		Ichinoseki Tora-Go	Kin-Go Tama-Go
	Saburo-Go		
		Oshinai-Go	Tochisan-Go Babagoma-Go
Arawashi-Go			
		Ichinoseki Tora-Go	Kin-Go Tama-Go
	Yama-Go		
		Kuma-Go	Tora-Go Aka-Go
		Dainidewa-Go	Raiden-Go Wakatoram-Go
	Araiwa-Go		
		Iwa-Go	Raiden-Go Akiba-Go
Sankatsu-Go			
		Shintora-Go	Toshigoro-Go Toshi-Go
	Fukuju-Go		
		Ichimaru-Go	Dainiteranishi-Go Hakuboatan-Go

The Meiyosho winning female Tamayu-Go, with Joan Linderman in Japan, 1970.

Toshime-Go, an outstanding brindle female Meiyosho winner.

Kincho-Go, bred by the well-known Mr. Abe.

30

DEWA-GO, whelped February 1, 1941
Owned by Mr. Yozaburo

		Aikoku-Go	Goma-Go
	Akagoro-Go		Aka-Go
		Shiro-Go	Katsura-Go
Akidate-Go			Tama-Go
		Taro-Go	(unknown)
	OtsutaGoma-Go		(unknown)
		Kuma-Go	(unknown)
			(unknown)
		Katsuhira-Go	(unknown)
	Mutsu-Go		(unknown)
		Goma-Go	(unknown)
Tama-Go			(unknown)
		Taka-Go	Ichinoseki Tora-Go
	Takatorame-Go		(unknown)
		Gin-Go	(unknown)
			(unknown)

31

KONGO-GO, born in 1947

		Dewa-Go	Akitate-Go
	Dewawaka-Go		Tama-Go
		Kuzugoma-Go	(unknown)
Taishu-Go			(unknown)
		Tokiwa-Go	Goma-Go
	Takahime-Go		Nagata-Go
		Maru-Go	Noritsu-Go
			Hayaguchigoma-Go
		Dewa-Go	Akitate-Go
	Dewawaka-Go		Tama-Go
		Kuzugoma-Go	(unknown)
Tatemitsu-Go			(unknown)
		Tategoro-Go	Tatetaro-Go
	Kikumaru-Go		(unknown)
		Tatetorama-Go	Habutaro-Go
			Tate-Go

3

The Early History
of the Akita in America

Contributions of American Servicemen

Why is the Akita in the United States? How did he reach our shores? Ironically, it took a war between two countries to bring him to our land. Servicemen stationed in Occupied Japan were captivated by his beauty; some simply wanted to bring home a "live" souvenir. A few who acquired Akitas entered them in the Japan Kennel Club all-breed show rings. Though showing was a hobby, some champions were made who, on return to the United States, were used in breeding programs.

Most of the first Akitas settled on our East and West coasts, destination points of ships returning home. California saw the largest influx of Akitas step foot on American soil. The state still boasts the greatest number of the breed as residents.

As our servicemen began to pick up the threads of their former lives, the animals they brought back quite naturally took a back seat in future plans. Even so, enough interest was aroused to create a market for more Akitas.

The breed grew slowly and much like "Topsy." In many instances, servicemen's families were unprepared for this new addition and ultimately sold or gave away their Akitas to people with more adequate facilities. Some of the Akitas were bred once, many were bred several times and some not at all.

It is unfortunate the Akita was brought here before Japanese fanciers began to make strides in improving the breed. Had Akitas come into the United States in the 1970's, the time when Mr. and Mrs. D. D. Confer and Karen Keene, military personnel, brought in the famous Grand Champions Haruhime and Teddy Bear of Toyohashi Seiko, we would possibly have had a better over-all, uniform type of dog here today.

Early Breed Clubs and Their Impact on the Breed

Our first breed clubs surfaced, disappeared and resurfaced. They changed their names, memberships, standards and club formats. Members were not professional dog breeders. For many, the Akita was their first dog. Material from Japan was not readily available. Breeding programs were a matter of guesswork. Culling was virtually unheard of. Few persons knew what to cull or how.

In 1952, the Akita Dog Association of America was established in Southern California and had a closed membership. Mr. M. Kelly Spellmeyer was founder and secretary.

On June 5, 1956, eleven Akita fanciers, who among them owned 30 Akitas, held the first general meeting of the second club organized, The Akita Kennel Club. Three years later, on September 6, 1959, it was suggested "Kennel" be omitted from the name. In November, 1959 steps were taken to achieve non-profit corporation status under the new name, "The Akita Club of America." Using forms patterned after those of the American Kennel Club, a registration file was set up for foreign and American-bred Akitas. Clyde Brown was President. Finally, on August 23, 1960, State of California papers were endorsed and filed. The parent club was born.

A month earlier, a splinter group from the club had started yet another new club, "Akita Breeders Association" with 14 charter members. On the heels of its formation, a letter

34

from attorney J. F. Cuneo informed them they were infringing on the rights of Mr. and Mrs. Lee Fisher who, on January 17, 1956, had the name Akita Breeders Association registered in Los Angeles County. However, we have no documented knowledge a working club was actually formed. The splinter group threw up its hands in exasperation and contacted Mr. Spellmeyer of Akita Dog Association of America. He agreed to open his closed membership to them.

The pot began to boil over. The new parent club accused Mr. Spellmeyer's new members of taking the Stud Book and missing registrations. According to our records, this was apparently resolved. In 1961 a newsletter, published by the Akita Club of America, Inc., contained within its pages, a motion made once again to accept the splinter group back into the fold of A.C.A. whose membership swelled to approximately 62.

As time passed, attempts were made to cement old relationships. However, in March, 1963, Charles W. Rubinstein led another group away from the parent club. Although Mr. Rubinstein left the scene and went on to other interests, the newly organized club named itself American Akita Breeders. Its membership boasted such well-knowns in Akitadom as Samuel and Barbara Mullen, William Conway, Anita Powell, Camille Kam.

The newly established A.A.B. added dimension and strength to the breed. Their shows were well organized. All had good attendance. Members remained unified until a short time before the Akita breed was recognized by the American Kennel Club.

Entered Miscellaneous Class at A.K.C. Shows

On July 13, 1955, the Akita was granted approval by A.K.C. to be shown in Miscellaneous Class at licensed all-breed shows. The records indicate the first Akitas shown in this class stepped into the ring on January 29, 1956 at the Orange Empire Kennel Club's fixture held in San Bernardino,

California. Mrs. Meyers judged. The records also indicate that 13 Akitas took part in 21 licensed shows and placed 50 times out of 168 possible placings their first year in Miscellaneous competition.

The first Akita ever shown in Miscellaneous Class at a prestigious Westminster Kennel Club show was Teruhime-Go, a red bitch who was brought into this country when she was 18 months old. She placed first. The press had a field day with "the unique breed from Japan." Owners Mr. and Mrs. Thomas Hamilton couldn't have been more proud.

Miscellaneous competition served as an apprenticeship for the Akita. Club point systems were set up for the animals who were shown. The judges were exposed to the breed and vice versa. Owners learned ring procedure and found out what it was like to have patience.

After 17 years in the Miscellaneous ring, our breed was finally recognized!

The Road to Recognition

That the road to recognition was filled with pot holes is quite obvious. When the bickering between the clubs reached a boiling point, new members with a fresh outlook said, "Enough is enough. Let's straighten out this mess!" An upheaval in the ranks ensued when questions pertaining to the validity of the registration bureau arose. Members demanded the right to have the Stud Book opened at general meetings, a reasonable request.

It had long been felt that one of the major stumbling blocks to recognition was the less than peaceful existence between the A.A.B. and the A.C.A.

Although attempts had been made to pull the two organizations together, it finally took a nine-person arbitration committee on October 4, 1969, to try and effect a merger. Walter Imai, representing the Japanese community, served as mediator. The goal was to create one united Akita club. The attempt was thwarted by factions within the A.C.A.

36

A short time later, some members of the A.C.A. formed "The Insight Group." Frederick W. Pitts, M.D., famous neurosurgeon, had an Akita and was persuaded to join the cause. The "Group" decided to present a slate of officers for the coming A.C.A. election which would bring about the needed merger and provide strict interpretation of club constitution and by-laws. Though election proceedings were unpleasant, the slate won. Club relations improved, A.C.A. and A.A.B. had a successful merger and a fair editorial policy was established for the newsletter.

On February 13, 1971, the club registrar resigned. President Pitts appointed a committee to take over. With Monica Vogl as Chairperson and President Pitts and three other members serving, the Stud Book comprised 3,082 entries after it was updated per American Kennel Club regulations. Kay Greisan eventually replaced Mrs. Vogl and stayed with the job until recognition.

According to President Pitts, "The credibility of our Stud Book is the life blood of this club, the purity of the Akita breed in this country and the key to recognition by the American Kennel Club. I believe the proposals I have outlined will re-establish confidence in the registration process."

1971 was an exciting year. John Brownell, Vice-President of A.K.C., met with Akita Club of America's board of directors. The workers kept working. A lot of paperwork was completed. But it was not until receipt of the following two letters that we knew recognition was totally ours.

THE AMERICAN KENNEL CLUB
51 MADISON AVENUE
NEW YORK, N.Y. 10010

October 24, 1972

NOTICE

REGISTRATION OF THE AKITA

By action of the Board of Directors of The American Kennel Club, the Akita has been admitted to registry in the AKC Stud Book, effective immediately.

Registration of Akitas now in the United States will generally be limited to dogs that have already been individually registered or litter registered with the Akita Club of America.

Special AKC registration application forms for the registration of foundation stock for the breed are available on request by writing to:

Mrs. Kay Greisen, Registrar   Mrs. Barbara Uyeda
Akita Club of America   Akita Club of America
P. O. Box 3742, University Station   1936 Armacost Avenue
Charlottesville, VA 22902   West Los Angeles, CA 90025

All such applications, when completed, must be mailed to Mrs. Greisen at the above address. Mrs. Greisen will forward them to The American Kennel Club.

For a dog from an ACA registered litter that has not been individually registered, the completed ACA registration form must be attached to the special application.

No fee will be required with a special application to register a dog that has been individually registered by the ACA -- the fee will be paid by ACA for such dogs. Check or money order for $3.00 must accompany each special application to register a dog from an ACA registered litter that has not yet been individually registered. The fee for registering an imported Akita whelped outside the U.S.A. that has not been registered with ACA will be $10.00.

If you have imported an Akita whelped outside the U.S.A. that has not yet been registered with ACA -- or if you intend to import an Akita -- write to the Registrar, Mrs. Greisen, for instructions, giving her the name of the dog's country of birth. The American Kennel Club plans to register Akitas imported from Japan under policies that conform with present ACA policies -- but only as long as The American Kennel Club Stud Book is open for the registration of foundation stock. Thereafter, the only imports that will be eligible for AKC registration will be those that meet regular American Kennel Club policies applying to imported dogs whelped outside the U.S.A.

AMERICAN KENNEL CLUB
51 MADISON AVENUE
NEW YORK, N. Y. 10010

WILLIAM F. STIFEL
EXECUTIVE SECRETARY

October 12, 1973

Mrs. Joan M. Linderman, President
Akita Club of America
18225 Sunburst Drive
Northridge, California 91324

Dear Mrs. Linderman:

Please be advised that by action of our Board of Directors at its recent meeting, the Stud Book will be closed to further registration of Akitas and Bichons Frises as foundation stock on February 28, 1974.

On and after March 1, 1974, Akitas and Bichons Frises will be registrable only under the regular registration procedures of The American Kennel Club.

Notice of this action will be published in the December 1973 and January 1974 issues of Pure-Bred Dogs American Kennel Gazette.

Very truly yours,

William F. Stifel
Executive Secretary

WFS:er
c.c. Mrs. Leajoan Schultz, Secretary
Mrs. Kay Greisen, Registrar

Akitas on Parade. The Royal Akita Club in San Francisco participates in the Cherry Blossom Festival, 1970.

Hozan-Go at the Beverly Riviera Show,
1960. Owner, Mr. and Mrs. Ivan Wong.

Teruhime-Go. Owners: Mr. and Mrs. T. Hamilton.

Aka Goma Jyo-Go

L. to R.—Akita Tani's Tora and her sire Akita Tani's Shoyo Go are pictured with Nancy Hoeltje.

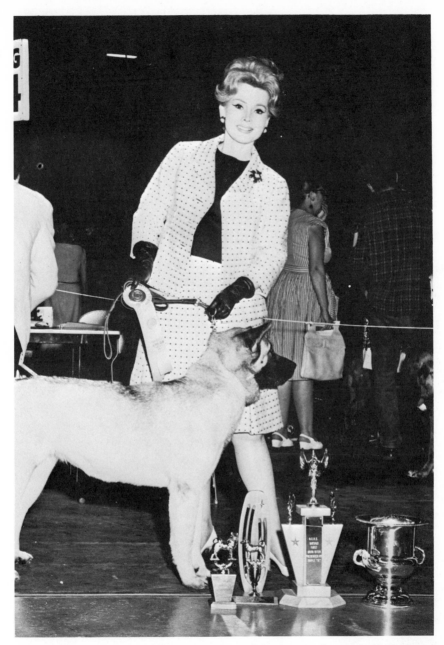

1963 Harbor Cities K.C. show saw Zsa Zsa Gabor with Triple "K" Ginsei Shimo. "Shimo's" owners, Mr. and Mrs. William Conway had reason to be proud.

Lil O'Shea's Issei Riki Oji-Go. A
marvelous brindle male, circa 1965.

Triple "K" Shina Ningyo and Marie Bevacqua,
Triple "K" Yo Ko and Camille Kam,
Triple "K" Ginsei Shimo and Kathy Conway. Circa 1960.

Mex. Ch. Triple "K" Miko and owner Dianne Russell, 1966. Miko's
sire was Mex. Ch. Triple "K" Hayai Taka, his dam was Mex. Ch.
Triple "K" Shina Ningyo.

4

Hall of Fame in America—Pedigree Studies

"When I judged in Japan in 1959, I told them I thought they had a great export commodity in the Akita."

—Maxwell Riddle

The Akita Club of America registry is numbered from 100 on. The male dog Nikko-Go, born March 13, 1952, is its first entry. He was brought into the United States by Lionel Fishman. Nikko was a combination of Ichinoseki and Dewa lines. Although we have no record of his being bred, his pictures portray him as being a well put together Akita.

The first stud to have an impact on early American breeding programs was Homare no Maiku-Go. Our records indicate he produced four litters, two out of breedings to Tamafugi-Go no Tokyo and one each resulting in breedings to Fukuchiyo-Go and Shunki Kodomo no Akita Ken. Homare was born on July 10, 1953 at the Shitara Kennel in Japan. Lee Fisher imported him. Homare's pedigree shows the Dewa line in his background. His undercoat was fawn. His outerlayer and guard hairs were black.

Homare bred to the import Fukuchiyo-Go produced the bitch Gin-Joo-Go of Triple "K." When bred to Mr. and Mrs. Guarino's import male, Grand Champion Kinsho-Go, she had in her litter three bitches, Akarui Kokoro, Triple "K" Shina Ningyo and Haiiro Kitsune. They were used extensively.

Mr. and Mrs. Lee Fisher arriving from Japan
with Homare no Maiku-Go and Tama.

HOMARE NO MAIKU-GO, whelped July 10, 1953
Owners Mr. and Mrs. Lee Fisher

Taro-Go	Araiwa-Go	Dainidewa-Go
		Iwa-Go
	Fukuju-Go	Shintaro-Go
		Ichimaru-Go
Ace Hashimoto	Kongo-Go	Taishu-Go
		Tatemitsu-Go
	Haname	Kinzan-Go
		Akitora-Go

TAMAFUJI-GO NO TOKYO, whelped Sept. 11, 1955
Owners Mr. and Mrs. Lee Fisher

Fujigoro-Go	Goromaru-Go	Ichinoseki Goma-Go
		Futatsuigoma-Go
	Fuji-Go	Oji-Go
		Kocho-Go
Kinki-Go	Kincho-Go	Kongo-Go
		Asahime-Go
	Kinterume-Go	Kincho-Go
		Teruhime-Go

Akarui Kokoro and Haiiro Kitsune were purchased by Mr. and Mrs. A. Harrell. When they bred Kokoro back to her sire Kinsho-Go, she produced Akita Tani's Shoyo-Go who, when bred back to his dam, gave them the highly inbred Akita Tani's Tatsumaki R.O.M.

Emma Jung purchased Triple "K" Shina Ningyo and mated her to Maru Kinsei no Suna-Go. One of the offspring, Triple "K" Ginsei Shimo was sold to Mr. William Conway who owned Triple "K" Shogo. These two produced Mexican Champion Kinsei Suna Nihon no Taishi C.D. He sired Mexican and American Champion Fukumoto's Ashibaya Kuma R.O.M.

When Walter Kam came home from Japan on the aircraft carrier U.S.S. Shangri-La, he brought with him Triple "K" Kennel's two foundation Akitas, Goronishiki-Go and the forementioned Fukuchiyo-Go whose first breeding brought forth the masculine Triple "K" Hayai Taka. When Hayai Taka was bred to Mr. and Mrs. Linderman's bitch Ichiban Mitsubachi C.D. she whelped the bitch Mexican Champion Sakusaku Gorotsuki-Go R.O.M., call name "Goro."

The Lindermans' famous American, Canadian, Mexican CACIB Champion Gin-Gin Haiyaku-Go of Sakusaku R.O.M. (Ch. Sakusaku's Tom Cat-Go R.O.M. x Mex. Ch. Shimi Kuma), known to Akita fanciers as "Chester," was not bred often. However, he had an outstanding show career. He was Best of Breed 200+ times and had over 50 group placings. His early show and breeding career was with Sakusaku Kennels, and later with Date Tensha Kennels on the East Coast.

Tom Cat's brother, Chester's maternal grandfather, the pinto import Toryu-Go (see photo, chapter 13) was of Goromaru lineage. Bred several times to Triple "K" Yoko (photo, chapter 3), he and his progeny are found in the pedigrees of many present-day Akitas.

Tom Cat's brother Champion Tusko's Kabuki had an outstanding show career. His sisters, Sakusaku's Tiger Lily and Tusko's Star, did well as producers.

Mr. Ed Strader brought Grand Champion Teruhide into

GORONISHIKI-GO, whelped June 5, 1956

		Shintora-Go
	Senzan-Go	Daininiyogetsu-Go
Taizan-Go		Hamatora-Go
	Kozakura-Go	Tomoe-Go
		Wakataro-Go
	Horyu-Go	Hatsuharu-Go
Sawahime-Go		Senko-Go
	Izuminohana-Go	Shirafuji-Go

FUKUCHIYO-GO, bitch whelped February 5, 1957
Owner, Camille Kam

		Odate-Go
---	Izuminokin-Go	Tamafuji-Go
Izuminotatsu-Go		Ichinoseki Goma-Go
	Dainikisaragi-Go	Matsukaze-Go
	Senzan-Go	Shintora-Go
Fujihime-Go		Dainikisaragi-Go
	Takahime-Go	Shintora-Go
		Teruhime-Go

Japanese Grand Champion KINSHO-GO,
whelped March 20, 1957
Owner at time of dog's death unknown

		Taishu-Go
	Kongo-Go	Tatehikari-Go
Kincho-Go		Hokkohu-Go
	Asahime-Go	Hakuho-Go
		Goromaru-Go
	Fudo-Go	Yohei-Go
Shirayuki-Go		Hideo-Go
	Yuki-Go	Ginrei-Go

Mr. and Mrs. R. Pattee's well-known Major and
Cindy, circa 1960.

MAJOR	Wakagimi	Daigo	Gomaiwa
			Mtsuhikari
		Kiyohime	Kodewa
			Shinichimaru
	Sachihime	Kodo	Fujiryu
			Harukaze
		Tamamo	Fuji
			Kitahime
CINDY	Kamikaze	Taiko Maru	Shingoma
			Chima
		Hamahime	Shinhama
			Shinhime
	Kiyome	Okin	Kincho
			Takahime
		Kiyoryu	Fudo
			Shintamazakura

this country on completion of his tour of duty. He garnered Teruhide's Japanese title while he and the dog were still in Japan. A well structured pinto, Teruhide was not a tall Akita but was within the standard for the breed. He eventually went to live with Mr. and Mrs. A. Harrell who bred him to Kogata Takara (Fuji Akashi x Kumiko). Parnassus Meiyo of Akita Tani, successful in the Miscellaneous ring, was from that breeding. When Meiyo was bred to Akita Tani's Shoyo-Go, the well-known male Akita Tani's Makoto was one of the whelps from that union.

The two males, the red Tochifuji and the red and white pinto Hozan were brought into the United States by their owners, Rocklaine Imports. After several changes of ownership, Tochifuji was acquired by Mr. and Mrs. Robert Judd. Hozan went to Ivan Wong. Tochifuji brought some Ichinoseki blood to our shores. Hozan had a brief, but brilliant show career. He was killed in an automobile accident.

With the half-brothers Tochifuji in California and Shiroi O Sama-Go on the East Coast, one would have expected some like offspring but it was not to be.

Shiroi O Sama-Go a.k.a. White King-Go Gobunso and Aka Goma Joo a.k.a. Jyo were the original O'Shea Akitas. Lil O'Shea had raised Pomeranians for 30 years prior to receiving White King for Christmas in 1962. She and her husband, William, later bought Jyo.

Three litters were produced by White King and Jyo. One of their most famous offspring was Issei Riki Oji-Go who, when bred to Kuma's Akai Kosho-Go out of Krug's Santo, produced Mitsu Kuma's Tora Oji-Go, a top winning male when the breed was first shown in licensed rings in 1973. Mitsu Kuma's Tora Oji-Go was the foundation male for Terry Wright's kennel in Maryland. She acquired him from Mr. and Mrs. Samuel Mullen in 1970.

The Mullens started their breeding program with the bitch Kuma Akai Kosho. When bred to the O'Sheas' Issei Riki Oji-Go they produced such Akitas as Mitsu Kuma's Splashdown, Mitsu Kuma's Moonbeam and the three Mitsu Kuma

Shunki Kodomo no Akita Ken
and the Jeffrye family.

Silver Crown Momo. Momo was bred by Lee
Simmons and owned by Marge Rutherford. Picture vintage 1959.

Yukihime-Go Bahi, owner George Hall. Yuki was produced at the famous Bahi Kennel of Mr. Hall in Japan.

Another Bahi great: Shiro Boke-Go Bahi.

Shiroi O-Sana-Go and Akagoma Jyo-Go.

SHIROI O-SANA-GO, whelped September 6, 1963
Owners, Mr. and Mrs. William O'Shea

	Tanihibiki-Go	Goromaru-Go
Tochihibiki-Go		Shiromaru-Go
	Kiyomaru-Go	Goromaru-Go
		Kaoru-Go
	Rikimaru-Go	Tanigumo-Go
Nisikigi-Go		Fujinime-Go
	Tanime-Go	Tanihibiki-Go
		Marunime-Go

Tochifuji and Robert Judd.

TOCHIFUJI, whelped February 18, 1962
Owner, Linda Judd Bruhn

		Coromaru-Go	Ichinoseki Coma-Go
	Tanihibiki-Go		Futatsuigoma-Go
		Shiromaru-Go	Todoroki-Go
Tochihibiki-Go			Mizuhataya-Go
		Goro-Go	Ichinoseki Coma-Go
	Kiyomaru-Go		Futatsuigoma-Go
		Kaoru-Go	Oji-Go
			Kochi-Go
		Gyokuun-Go	Arawashi-Go
	Goro-Go		Sansho-Go
		Yuki-Go	Goromaru-Go
Tamafuji-Go			Chiyohana-Go
		Ryuo-Go	Kongo-Go
	Kii-Go		Tachibana-Go
		Aimi-Go	Shinmatsumine-Go
			Uryuhime-Go

57

champions Tora, Tiki and Kash.

A lot of today's East Coast dogs have the dog Prince Jo C.D. and the bitch Sheba in their pedigrees. Prince Jo was the foundation dog for the Sakura Kennels of Mr. and Mrs. Robert Miller. A breeding to Michiko of Kensha C.D. gave them their Champion Sakura's Bushi C.D. Sheba, owned by Mr. and Mrs. Francis Krug, whelped Krug's Santo as a result of her breeding to Goyokushu of Tojo. When Santo was bred to the bitch import Karatachi, Krug's Sotto, a well-known male, was the result. Both Santo and Sotto were used frequently on the East Coast.

Ketket's Tiger Bear C.D. and Kanpuzan-Go were two imports who had an impact on the breed in America in the 1970's. Tiger Bear sired Kitamaru who has contributed greatly to the breed in the midwest. Kanpuzan-Go was bred to Champion Triple "K" Chiyo. Out of this union came Champion Triple "K" Shoyu-Go C.D. Shoyu in turn sired Champion Hashi's Satoshi Awoyama. This young male just passed away tragically. Bred only a few times his still youthful progeny show great promise.

Breeding activity in the United States has been lively since recognition. We have not, however, dwelled on famous kennels or famous personalities within our breed for a reason. The Akita dog has not been in this country long enough to give accolades.

Japanese Champion Tosaryu-Go, owned by Anita Powell, is shown with Miss Denmark, Alice Bjorn Anderson.

Mexican Champion Triple "K" Hayai Taka-Go
(Goronishiki-Go x Fukuchiyo-Go) and Emma Jung.

Triple "K" Arashi-Go, brother of Triple "K" Hayai Taka.

Mexican Champion Triple
"K" Shina Ningyo.

Triple "K" Shogo and Triple "K" Shimo and
litter. Owners Mr. and Mrs. William Conway.

The famous Japanese Grand Champion Haruhime. Her family, Nancy, Ginger, Barbara and Don Confer, called her "Kita." Her pedigree appears below.

		Toun	Azumazakura
	Tensei		Gyokurei
		Fumihime	Ichitaro
			Meigyoku
		Yoshitora	Tengai
	Otorahikarijo		Fujihime
		Mutsuhime	Hataryumaru
			Kahoru

Japanese Grand Champion
TEDDY BEAR OF TOYOHASHI SEIKO
whelped September 13, 1965
Owner, Mrs. Karen Keen

		Hachi	Kuma-Go
	Dai of Garyusu		Terumaru-Go
		Hatsume	Jiro-Go
Daio of Toyohashi Seiko			Manryu-Go
		Seibun	Ayahikari-Go
	Aruma of Toyohashi		Shakauchi-Go
	Seiko	Yukihime	Tetsumaro-Go
			Fukusumi-Go
		Seibun	Ayahikari-Go
	Taiho of Mikawa		Shakauchi-Go
	Asahi	Ayame	Seibun
Shuri of Mikawa Asahi			Yukihime-Go
		Dai of Garyuso	Hachi-Go
	Mutsuhime of		Hatsume-Go
	Toyohashi Seiko	Aruma of Toyohashi	Seibun
		Seiko	Yukihime-Go

64

Mexican and American Champion Fukumoto's
Ashibaya Kuma and breeder Diane Russell, in
1968.

Mexican Champion Kinsei Suna Nihon no Taishi (Triple "K" Shogo x Triple "K" Ginsei Shimo.

Champion Toyo no Charlie Brown, bred by the Confers and owned by Carol Foti

Champion Kuro Panzu Maru No Asagaa (Ch. Sakura's Bushi C.D. x Ch. Krug's Shumi Go Ditmore).

66

Yukan no Okii Yubi R.O.M. (Fukumoto's Ashibaya Kuma x Toyo no Namesu Joo), owner Robert Campbell.

Champion Okii Yubi Sachmo of Makoto R.O.M. Now deceased, this champion sired over 70 champions. Breeder, Robert Campbell. Owners, Mr. and Mrs. William Andrews.

Anne Diener with Champion Sakusaku's Diamond Lil. One of the early champions, she finished April 29, 1973.

Sakusaku's Daffodil Lil at four months with Sue Sanett.

A top winning male in the midwest, Champion Cee-Jays Chumley P. Linderman is shown with owner Ben Tomazewski.

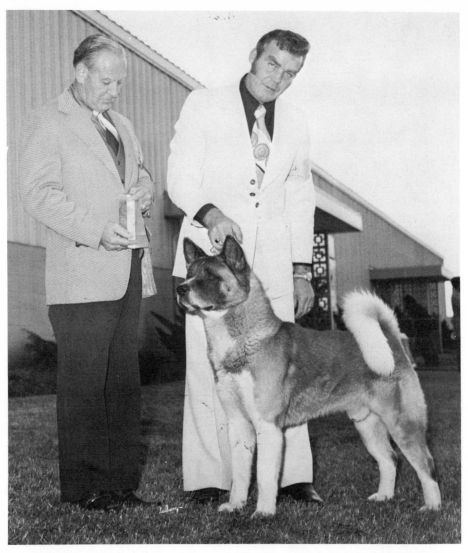

Champion Kin Ko, import owned by Mr. and Mrs. Harold Hunt.

Champion Tusko's Kabuki (Japanese Gr. Ch. Teddy Bear of Toyohashi Seiko x Japanese Gr. Ch. Haru Hime) is shown with owner Dr. Peter Lagus.

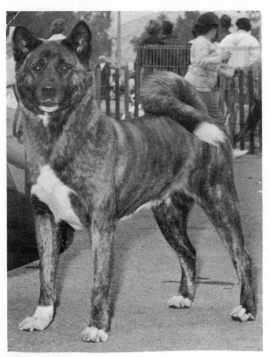

Sakusaku's Tiger Lily (Japanese Gr. Ch. Teddy Bear of Toyohashi Seiko x Japanese Gr. Ch. Haru Hime).

Tomonobu-Go. Owned by Mr. and Mrs. Kenji Y. Kusumoto, he was one of the last imports which was able to be registered in the American Kennel Club.

5

The Breed Standard in America

Background of the Modern Standard

IN ORDER TO UNDERSTAND how today's Akita Standard in America came to be, we must go back to Japan and trace its long journey from East to West.

The beauty and magnificence of the Japanese Akita breed was laid out for us in the early 1930's. There were at this time in Japan, several all-Japanese breed organizations in existence. In the beginning they used the same Standard of Reference. Some have said the dog organization NIPPO wrote the first one. However, it is the Standard put forth by the Akitainu Hozonkai Organization (AKIHO), whose people are dedicated students of the history of the breed, which interests us deeply. It is used by judges at the annual AKIHO Branch Show in Los Angeles, enabling us to see how the Akita and its appearance have been preserved.

The Standard itself is comparatively brief. It is accompanied by an in-depth translation by Mr. Walter Imai, past Chairman of AKIHO, Los Angeles Branch. Mr. Imai's expertise as translator stems from 11 years schooling in Japan and as an interpreter for the United States Army plus his present role as president of his own import/export corporation. He has owned two outstanding Akitas but does not consider himself a breeder. Even so, his knowledge of dog terminology was essential for correct translation from Japanese to English.

AKITAINU STANDARDS

Adopted September 18, 1955

CHARACTERISTICS

An Akita is quiet, strong, dignified and courageous. He is also loyal and respectful, reserved and noble. He is sensitive and deliberate yet possesses quickness.

OVER-ALL BODY STRUCTURE

The body is well balanced with a sturdy bone structure and well developed tendons and ligaments while the skin is free of wrinkles. Differences in sex should be readily apparent through general appearance. In the dog (male) the ratio of height to body length is 100 to 110. The bitch is slightly longer in length. The height of the dog is 26¼ inches while the height of the bitch is 23⅞ inches, plus or minus 1⅛ inches. The ratio of the height to the depth of the chest is 2 to 1.

HEAD

The skull is large and a little flat at the top. Its forehead is wide without wrinkles but has a definite longitudinal crease. There is a well proportioned *stop* (depression between the cranial and nasal bones) between the forehead and the muzzle. The cheeks are full.

NECK

The neck is thick and powerful. The skin around the neck is free of wrinkles and the coat appropriately bristled.

EAR

The ears are thick, rather small, triangular in shape, and tilt slightly forward. The lines are straight and the ears stand erect. The distance between the ears is not narrow but not too wide.

EYES

The shape of the eye is approximately triangular. They are deep-set and slightly slanted. The eye-rims are dark-brownish in color. The distance between the eyes is proportionate.

MUZZLE (Mouth and Nose)

The nose (black portion) is full and the ridge straight. The base of the mouth is wide, the frontal portion not pointed, and the lips drawn. The whiskered region is full.

TEETH

The teeth are strong and have a scissor bite.

CHEST AND STOMACH

The chest is broad. The rib cage is full. The forechest is well developed and defined. The stomach is drawn without flabbiness (tucked up).

BACK AND HIP

The back is straight and the hip is powerful.

FORELEGS (Arms)

The shoulders are well developed with proper shoulder angulation. The elbows (joint) are strong. The upper forelegs are straight, strong and thick. The *pasterns* (portion directly above paws) are slightly slanted. The paws are round, large, and thick, and have a firm grip.

HIND LEGS

The hind legs are well developed, springy, powerful and sturdy. The rear pasterns have proper angles and possess a strong kick or thrust. The paws are thick with a strong grip.

TAIL

The tail is thick and tightly wound. The length of the tail when extended must reach the hock joint. The types of curls are called right curl, left curl, single straight, and double curl.

COAT

The outer coat is coarse and straight, while the under-coat is fine and thick. The coat at the withers (shoulder region) and rump is slightly longer than the rest of the body. The tail has the longest coat.

COLOR OF COATS: White, black, red, silver-tipped, brindle and pinto.

MINOR FAULTS

1. Permanent injury and dietary deficiency.
2. Color of coat unbecoming to an Akita.
3. Undesirable color combination of coat and eye-rim.
4. Loss of tooth or teeth. Undershot and overshot jaws.
5. Black spotting on tongue.
6. Lacking in courage, being timid, or displaying ferociousness or otherwise lacking the qualities suitable for Akitas.

MAJOR FAULTS

1. Floppy ears by birth (ears failing to stand).
2. Straight tail by birth.
3. Excessively long or short coat.
4. Color of nose not matching the color of coat. (Reddish

or pink nose acceptable with white coat).

5. Bilateral or unilateral cryptorchidism.

6. Other defects detracting from the qualities of Akitas.

An Analysis of the Akitainu Hozonkai Standard for the Akita

(Written by the research committee of the Akitainu standard in Japan, with the use of historical records. Translated from the Japanese by Walter Imai, chairman, Akitainu Hozonkai, Los Angeles branch.)

Introduction: *The Akita Character*

The term "character," as applied to an animal, is not easy to define. Our analysis of the Akita's character is traditional and historical, drawn from what has been passed on to us from the older generation, and from our own experiences with the breed, as well as from written material and literature from years past.

An Akita has quiet strength, dignity and courage. An Akita is large, with a powerful bone structure as the foundation of the body. The dog's sheer size, combined with its regal bearing, gives it the aura of being "king of all dogs."

An Akita's nature is to be intensely loyal to its master. This is especially strong in the Akita compared to other breeds. This characteristic parallels the intensely loyal character of the traditional Japanese people.

An Akita's outward appearance, reflecting the inner nature, is calm but at the same time very brave. While the Akita does not challenge first, neither does it back down from the challenge of another.

The character is not an aspect of the Akita that we can measure with a yardstick. Nevertheless it is a fundamental and most important aspect of the breed. Call it what you will— class, pride, bearing—it must be present for a dog to be a good Akita.

A. Overall Structure

The structure of the body governs the capabilities of the Akita. The structure is seen by examining the dog's basic parts and organs and its basic movements. It involves the height, length, weight, and general appearance of the dog.

The bone structure must be powerful, tight, and well-balanced. Muscles, tendons and ligaments must be well-developed and strong. Such development must be accompanied by natural beauty. If an Akita does not possess a well-developed structure, the dog is sloppy, loose jointed, without balance, and physically weak.

The torso is divided into the front section, the mid-section, and the hind section. If the proportions of these sections are not proper, the Akita in its standing position will not look right because it will not have the balance that it requires. Furthermore, its movements will not be smooth, and therefore the dog will not possess staying power. The proper proportions of the sections determine the balance of the structure of the torso.

(The location of the front, mid-, and hind sections is as follows: looking at the dog's profile in a normal standing posture, the front section extends from the front of the chest or brisket to an imaginary vertical line drawn through the point of the elbow. The mid-section extends from this line to another imaginary vertical line drawn through the point where the dog's hind leg intersects with the body. The hind section extends from this second vertical line to the back of the haunch. *author's note*)

1. The ratio of the torso sections to each other in length: (front) 1.0 to (mid-) 1.4 to (hind) 1.0.

2. Depth of chest is 55% of the height of the dog. Example: At the ideal height of 66.7 centimeters (26¼ inches), the depth of chest should ideally be 36.9 cm. (14½ in.), or between an upper limit of 37.0 cm. (14½ in.) and a lower limit of 33.4 cm. (13¼ in.).

3. Chest circumference is 23% greater than the height of the dog. Example: At the ideal height of 66.7 cm., circumference of the chest should ideally be 81.8 cm. (32¼ in.), or between an upper limit of 84.8 cm. (33½ in.) and a lower limit of 78.8 cm. (31 in.).

4. Width of the chest is 44% as great as the height of the dog. Example: At the ideal height of 66.7 cm., width of the chest should ideally be 29.0 cm. (11½ in.), or between an upper limit of 30.7 cm. (12 in.) and a lower limit of 28.1 cm. (11 in.).

5. Width of the hips is 40% as great as the height of the dog. Example: At the ideal height of 66.7 cm., width through the hips should ideally be 27.0 cm. (10½ in.), or between an upper limit of 28.0 cm. (11 in.) and a lower limit of 25.3 cm. (10 in.).

6. Weight: At the ideal height of 66.7 cm. (26¼ in.), the Akita should ideally weigh 45 kilograms (99 pounds).

(Measurements are rounded off to the nearest ¼ inch. Those who wish may make their own conversions from the more precise metric units given. Divide centimeters by 2.54 to get inches. Multiply kilograms by 2.2 to get pounds. *Author's note)*

The relationship of the depth of chest and the stomach is as follows: the chest and the stomach form a gentle curve, with the stomach severely tucked up towards the hips.

The relationship of body length to back and hip is as follows: The back is the portion of the topline between the shoulder blade and the loin. The length of the back is one-third the length of the body and should be level. Example: at the ideal length of body of 79.86 cm. (31½ in.), the back should measure 23.96 cm. (9½ in.).

The ratio of height of dog to depth of chest called for in the standard is two to one. However, because the desirable cross section of the chest is rather triangular in shape, it is best to have a somewhat deeper chest; thus the statement that depth of chest is 55% of the height of the dog. An Akita with a short back would have a deeper chest and wider shoulders, and the cross section of the chest would be rather round in shape.

The height, depth of chest, and all other measurements of the bitch are less than those of the dog.

B.　The Withers

The withers is the area that connects the neck with the shoulder blade, the shoulder and the chest. There is a slight indentation where the withers joins the back. An Akita with a high base of neck will have a weak back. A low base, on the other hand, will give a powerful back but impeded movement of the front legs.

C.　The Legs

The legs support the body of the Akita. Because they must initiate, generate, and withstand the shock that the movements create, they must be powerfully constructed and at the same time have much springiness. The cross section of the legs is approximately round. This is necessary for withstanding the various moves and shocks, and for supporting the dog's weight.

D.　The Shoulder

The shoulder blades form the base of the shoulders. Strong tendons connect the front legs to the front section of the torso at the shoulder blades. The shoulder blade is long and wide and must move freely. It moves back and forth about 10 to fifteen degrees. When the Akita is standing naturally, the shoulder blade is at an angle of 55 degrees to the ground.

The longer the shoulder blade, the more it slants, and the shorter it is, the more upright it is. Akitas with long shoulder blades have longer steps, and they are faster.

The shoulder blades should not protrude much from the chest, nor should they recede into it. They should turn neither in nor out.

E. The Upper Arm and Foreleg

The upper arm is constructed of the humerus, which is long in relation to the shoulder blade. It is parallel with the center of the torso. The angulation of the humerus and the shoulder blade is 110 to 120 degrees. If this angulation is less than 110 degrees, the forelegs are drawn back and the chest will protrude. If the humerus is too long, the dog's step will be low, and if it is too short the step will be high.

From the front, the humerus is perpendicular to the ground.

The forelegs must be parallel, but they should open slightly at the pastern. A vertical line from the point of the shoulder should divide the foreleg approximately in half.

From the side, a vertical line through the withers should barely touch the elbow.

F. Pastern and Grip

The pastern serves to cushion the impact of the dog's movement. If it slants to a large degree, it will not support the dog's weight well, but if it is upright it will not absorb the shock received by the leg. In either case, the dog's normal movement will be impaired. In the Akita, the proper angulation of the pastern to a line perpendicular to the ground is 10 to 15 degrees.

Also in the Akita, the grip has been considered very important from years back. The paws should be large, round and thick, without spacing between the toes. The color of the pad should be black. A liver-colored pad indicates lack of pigment in the whole body (lips, eyerims, etc.). The nails should be short and powerful. As in the case of the pad, the nails should be dark in color.

G. Hind Leg

The front legs support the weight of the body and change the direction of movement. The hind legs start and propel the move. Therefore, the upper thigh must be broad and powerful and have strong muscles. The bones—femur, fibula and tibia—are long. The angulation of these bones has been deemed extremely important from the very beginning of the breed. When the dog is standing normally, a vertical line from the back of the rump should touch on the back of the hock joint. The metatarsal bone should be parallel to the same vertical line.

The upper thigh must be full, with strong muscle development. It must be wide, long and thick. The length gives the dog its speed, the width its power. The angle between the pelvic bone and the femur is 80 to 100 degrees. The longer the femur, the more pronounced is the angulation. The more pronounced angulation and the longer bones produce the longer gait. Conversely, the less pronounced angulation would mean a shorter bone and a shorter gait.

The lower thigh is also very important to the movement of the dog. The angulation of the tibia to the femur is 110 to 125 degrees. The fibula and tibia should be supported firmly by ligaments and tendons. The longer the fibula and tibia, the more pronounced is the angulation to the metatarsus, which is normally 140 to 145 degrees.

When the Akita is in a normal standing position, the hock joint as viewed from the rear can be bisected by a vertical line that goes through the point of the rump. Hock joints that turn in or out are faulty.

Viewed from the side, a wide angle of the hock joint (called straight hock) would be weak in generating movement. On the other hand, if the angle is too sharp (called bent hock), the metatarsus is too sharply angled with the ground and cannot support the dog's body weight. In either case, the dog will lack stamina.

H. Anus

The anus should not protrude, but should be large and tight.

I. Tail

The tail consists of the trunk of the tail and its hair. It expresses the character of the dog and is also the rudder in the movement of the body. It should be thick, and can be either round or flat. The curl should be powerful and can be carried on the left or right rump or even in a double curl.

The *length* of the tail in extended position is specified as reaching the hock joint. However, the position of the hock joint in terms of the height of the dog varies enough so that a more absolute standard is desirable (the joint has become lower in recent years). Therefore the Akita's tail length should be two-thirds of the body height of the Akita.

Unlike the other Japanese canine breeds, *the Akita has an absolute requirement that the tail be wound.* Furthermore, the shape and type of the tail influence the value and character of the Akita. It is very important that the tail add to the regal bearing and brave character of the Akita. This is especially important today, because the Akita is primarily a show dog.

A tail that is thick would require more than a single curl, as it would lack strength at the tip. However, if a tail is thin, the curl may be shaped well, but the curl itself will be small. On the other hand, a large curl with a thin tail will lack the necessary dignity.

Generally speaking, the tail of a dog is based higher on the back than that of a bitch. This is so because of the dog's more aggressive nature. Furthermore, the hip bone of the bitch is large and is structured in such a way as to make its tail set lower.

J. Head

It has been passed on to modern times from years ago that in judging an Akita the structure of the head is important above all, as it houses the brain, which is the origin of all the actions of the dog.

The first requirement is that the *size* of the head be in balance with the size of the body. The size of the head, supported by the neck, influences the center of gravity (the balance) of the Akita. Generally speaking, one of the outstanding features of the Akita compared to the other Japanese breeds (Inu, Shiba, Hokaido Dog, etc.) is that the head is large.

The *shape* of the head from directly above is approximately triangular. The *length* of the head is approximately 9/22 of the height of the body (41%). The *thickness* of the head at its largest point is approximately one-half the length of the head.

The *skull* is comprised of the frontal and the rear skulls. The frontal skull (forehead) is wide, and the rear skull (back of the ears) must be well-developed, in a way peculiar to the Akita head. An undersized rear skull thus is lacking in one of the distinct features of the Akita.

An old saying in the annals of Akita literature is that "the neck is long and the jaw wide." A short neck is undesirable because it would tend to restrict the dog's movements.

The *forehead* is formed by the frontal skull. It is broad and only slightly rounded. The forehead must be broad because its development is related to the development of the brain.

The *vertical crease* running down the center of the forehead is shallow but must be distinct. An indistinguishable crease or a round forehead without the crease would be considered totally unlike the Akita of past or present.

The *stop* has a direct bearing on the quality of the facial expression. It should be pronounced. The stop is formed by the meeting of the forehead and the bridge of the nose. Viewed from the side, it gives the Akita its distinct appearance and is very important. However, when the stop is too pronounced it will show a more than strong character and even indicate a violent nature. The side view should show the frontal skull and the bridge of the nose to be parallel.

K.   *The Eyes*

The eyes are *approximately triangular* in shape, and they are *deep-set. The eye rim must be dark brown. The eyes are*

84

slightly slanted. As it is said of all animals, the eyes express the nature, disposition and feelings of the Akita. The size and position, and the distance between the eyes, are relative to the size of the head.

Together with the stop and the vertical crease, the eyes make up the facial expression of the Akita and are one of the important factors in the overall quality of the breed.

L. The Mouth

The mouth is comprised of the upper and lower jaw, including the teeth. Because its function is to chew as well as to bite, it is powerfully constructed and requires some width and depth. When viewed from the side, the line of the mouth forms a ninety degree angle with the front end of the nose. The mouth extends to the corner of the upper jaw, and its width is the width of the muzzle. Although the mouth has to be powerful, it must not be so large or powerful that it detracts from the noble look of the facial features.

M. Nose

The muzzle starts from the lower part of the forehead and extends to the black portion of the nose. The front part of the nose is large compared to other canine breeds. It is square in shape. Because it possesses the important sense of smell, the nose must be well-shaped and tight.

N. The Lips

The lips are drawn tightly, paralleling the jaw bones. They should not be flabby, but just full enough to cover the teeth.

O. The Teeth

Generally speaking, a dog of sturdy bone structure with large paws must have large, powerful teeth. The Akita is no exception. Because in its wild state the Akita had to fight other animals and also maintain good health, it has exceptionally long, sharp and strong teeth compared to the other native Japanese breeds of dog.

The scissor bite is the only acceptable bite. Among the teeth, the four canine teeth especially must be powerful and have proper bite.

P.   The Ears

It is said that if the eyes are the mirror of the heart, the ears are the heart's windows. The noble bearing of the Akita is greatly enhanced by the proper shape, quality and position of the dog's ears.

Like other Japanese purebreds, the Akita has a stand-up ear, showing alertness. When the dog is not feeling well or when it is not up to the occasion, it will flatten its ears.

The quality, shape, position and size of the ears must balance with the size and shape of the head and face. Ears that are too thick give the appearance of insensitivity; therefore, the ears should only be rather thick.

The standard says the ears must be approximately triangular. The tips should be slightly rounded rather than pointed, indicating the gentleness of the Akita.

As to position of the ear, when viewed from the front as the dog stands erect and looks straight ahead, a vertical line through the tip of the ear must divide the ear equally in half.

The standard calls for ears "rather small," but here again size must be relative to the size of the head. When folded forward, the tip of the ear should touch the eyelid. Viewed from the front, the highest part of the outer edge of the ear should be in line with the outside corner of the eye. The distance between the tips of the ears is 75% of the width of the face.

Q.   The Neck

Because the neck houses the windpipe, the throat must be appropriately thick and long. The skin that covers the neck *must* be tight. The muscles in the neck must be strong and powerful, so that the heavy head is supported for quick and free movement. When the Akita is carrying something in its mouth, the neck must be strong enough to support the weight. In order to properly exercise its sense of smell, the Akita must be able to move its head swiftly. In case of a fight, the neck is the most vulnerable part of the body.

When the neck is long, the shoulder blade tilts more, allowing longer steps and faster movement. However, when the neck is too long the head cannot be stable, and in general the dog is weaker. Its appearance will also lack dignity.

R. *The Coat*

The coat of the Akita has three distinct layers: the outer guard coat, the regular coat, and the woolly undercoat.

The *undercoat* is a thick, fine, cotton-like coat. It thins out during the summer months, but it is heavy during the winter to keep the body warm.

The *regular coat* is made of coarse hair, very resilient. The regular coat protects the body from injuries and repels water.

The *outer guard coat* is about 1.5 cm. (½ in.) longer than the regular coat and stands out like needles.

The *whiskers* are permanent; therefore, they are believed to have feeling, unlike the hair of the coat.

The Akita coat must be stiff and *open*. In rain and snow, it should not get soaking wet. If the coat is soft, the body will get completely wet.

How the Present Breed Standard Evolved

Most imports brought into the United States by returning servicemen and some enterprising souls after World War II were not good representatives of the breed. Most lacked type, structure, color and, frequently, ideal temperament. Japanese breeders wisely kept the "cream of the crop" for themselves.

Study of the Akita Club of America's Stud Book reveals that until the early '70s few fine specimens were either not used or not used to their potential. Many new Akita owners of the time lacked a thorough knowledge of the heredity of their dogs.

The first Breed Standard, as accepted by American Kennel Club and proposed by A.C.A. in 1960, specified "A head free from wrinkle," "Coat of almost any color from cream to black" (all-white was omitted), "Neck without excessive dewlap," "Size: Dogs 25½" to 27½" or more at the shoulder with bitches slightly smaller," "Weight in proportion to size, usually 85 to 110 pounds for dogs, 75 to 90 pounds for bitches." Disqualifying faults were not noted at end of Standard.

In 1963, after much study and concern, the Standard Committee submitted a revised "Standard of Perfection" to members of the Akita Club of America which those present approved. It was better written than the first Standard and contained important additions and deletions. The most dramatic changes were: Height: "Males, 25" to 28" or more; Bitches, 23" to 26" or more" with no mention of weight. Colors were specified as "Solids, Brindles, Pintos, Whites." Most important change here was the addition of White. "Solid white dogs may have a liver nose but the black nose is more desirable." Head: ". . . free from wrinkle *when at ease*." Stop: added to the original, "A stop well marked but not abrupt" were the words: "The furrow extends well up the forehead." Faults were included as follows:

MINOR—*Undesirable*	MAJOR—*Disqualifying*
a. Round or light eyes	a. Drop or broken ears
b. Excessive dewlap	b. Deafness
c. Dark spots on tongue	c. Uncurled tail
d. Coarseness in bitches	d. Altering length of coat
e. Over refinement in males	e. Shyness, viciousness or
f. Looseness	instability
g. Lack of spirit	f. "Pink" eye rims or lips
	g. Butterfly nose

In October, 1965, another Proposed Standard suggested weight of Akitas should be: "Males—90 to 140 pounds generally; Bitches—70 to 100 pounds generally."

In 1972, much controversy prevailed among parent club

members regarding the Standard of Perfection for Akitas as it should be written in order to gain recognition for the breed with the American Kennel Club. The question of size dominated.

On December 12, 1972, the Board of Directors of the American Kennel Club approved the following Standard for Akitas which became effective April 4, 1973 and as of this writing remains as written:

THE OFFICIAL STANDARD

GENERAL APPEARANCE—Large, powerful, alert, with much substance and heavy bone. The broad head, forming a blunt triangle, with deep muzzle, small eyes and erect ears carried forward in line with back of neck, is characteristic of the breed. The large, curled tail, balancing the broad head, is also characteristic of the breed.

HEAD—Massive but in balance with body; free of wrinkle when at ease. Skull flat between ears and broad; jaws square and powerful with minimal dewlap. Head forms a blunt triangle when viewed from above. Fault-Narrow or snipy head.

Muzzle—Broad and full. Distance from nose to stop is to distance from stop to occiput as 2 is to 3. *Stop*—Well defined, but not too abrupt. A shallow furrow extends well up forehead.

Nose—Broad and black. Liver permitted on white Akitas, but black always preferred. Disqualification—Butterfly nose or total lack of pigmentation on nose.

Ears—The ears of the Akita are characteristic of the breed. They are strongly erect and small in relation to rest of head. If ear is folded forward for measuring length, tip will touch upper eye rim. Ears are triangular, slightly rounded at tip, wide at base, set wide on head but not too low, and carried slightly forward over eyes in line with back of neck. Disqualification—Drop or broken ears.

Eyes—Dark brown, small, deep-set and triangular in shape. Eye rims black and tight.

Lips and Tongue—Lips black and not pendulous; tongue pink.

Teeth—Strong with scissors bite preferred, but level bite acceptable. Disqualification—Noticeably undershot or overshot.

NECK AND BODY

Neck—Thick and muscular; comparatively short, widening gradually toward shoulders. A pronounced crest blends in with base of skull.

Body—Longer than high, as 10 is to 9 in males; 11 to 9 in bitches. Chest wide and deep; depth of chest is one-half height of dog at shoulder. Ribs well sprung, brisket well developed. Level back with firmly-muscled loin and moderate tuck-up. Skin pliant but not loose. *Serious Faults*—Light bone, rangy body.

TAIL—Large and full, set high and carried over back or against flank in a three-quarter, full, or double curl, always dipping to or below level of back. On a three-quarter curl, tip drops well down flank. Root large and strong. Tail bone reaches hock when let down. Hair coarse, straight and full, with no appearance of a plume. *Disqualification*—Sickle or uncurled tail.

FOREQUARTERS AND HINDQUARTERS

Forequarters—Shoulders strong and powerful with moderate layback. Forelegs heavy-boned and straight as viewed from front. Angle of pastern 15 degrees forward from vertical. *Faults*—Elbows in or out, loose shoulders.

Hindquarters—Width, muscular development and comparable to forequarters. Upper thighs well developed.

90

Stifle moderately bent and hocks well let down, turning neither in nor out.

Dewclaws—On front legs generally not removed; dewclaws on hind legs generally removed.

Feet—Cat feet, well knuckled up with thick pads. Feet straight ahead.

COAT—Double-coated. Undercoat thick, soft, dense and shorter than outer coat. Outer coat straight, harsh and standing somewhat off body. Hair on head, legs and ears short. Length of hair at withers and rump approximately two inches, which is slightly longer than on rest of body, except tail, where coat is longest and most profuse. *Fault*—Any indication of ruff or feathering.

COLOR—Any color including white; brindle; or pinto. Colors are brilliant and clear and markings are well balanced, with or without mask or blaze. White Akitas have no mask. Pinto has a white background with large, evenly placed patches covering head and more than one-third of body. Undercoat may be a different color from outer coat.

GAIT—Brisk and powerful with strides of moderate length. Back remains strong, firm and level. Rear legs move in line with front legs.

SIZE—Males 26 to 28 inches at the withers; bitches 24 to 26 inches. Disqualification—Dogs under 25 inches; bitches under 23 inches.

TEMPERAMENT—Alert and responsive, dignified and courageous. Aggressive toward other dogs.

DISQUALIFICATIONS

Butterfly nose or total lack of pigmentation on nose.
Drop or broken ears.

Noticeably undershot or overshot.
Sickle or uncurled tail.
Dogs under 25 inches; bitches under 23 inches.

CONCLUSION

Everyone has his own idea of what the perfect Akita should be like. Breeding laws and theories are useless unless one can recognize the correct Akita type, its structure, gait and temperament.

The authors of this book are aware that attempts to revise our present Standard have been made. We also know there are constant movements afoot to "loosen" the uncurled tail disqualification. In our opinion, the distinguishing characteristics of a breed should never be diluted. A regrettable example of the standard being changed to fit the dog is the degeneration of the statement "A head free of wrinkle" to "A head free of wrinkle when at ease."

Akita owners carry the responsibility for the future of the breed. They should face what lies ahead with open minds and tolerance and not be intimidated by a so-called powerful minority whose dogs do not measure up.

It is a pity Walter Imai's translation and analysis of the Japanese Standard was not made earlier than the 1970's. How different things would be today!

6

The Akita Dog—An Anatomy

Proportion

The male dog's height to body length ratio is 100 to 110. The bitch is a trifle longer in length.

Head

"An Akita's head is a symphony of triangles."
—Joan Linderman in *Kennel Review*

Although the head is in balance with the body it is large in appearance. The wide, slightly rounded forehead has no wrinkles. Two important traits not to be overlooked are the distinct vertical crease down the center of the forehead and the full, full cheeks. The nose should be large, black and pretty much square-shaped. It should be a healthy nose. The white Akita may have a liver colored nose. Dog's head should show masculinity; the bitch's, femininity.

Ears

The stand up ear is fairly small and triangular in shape. It is broad at the base, slightly rounded at the tip and thick enough not to show weakness. The inner part of the ear is sheltered by the forward (45°) angle or tilt over the eyes.

Because ears are a distinguishing characteristic, they are extremely important.

Eyes

Deep set, dark brown color and almost triangular in shape. They are slightly slanted. The eye rims are dark and tight. There must be no sagging of the lower rim. This is a stressed characteristic. Breeders and judges must adhere to a correct eye.

Mouth

Powerful in structure with tight black lips and large, powerful teeth in a proper scissor bite is to be preferred. All four canine teeth should be present. Preference is to no black spots on the tongue.

Neck

Tightly covered by skin, it must be well-muscled and not too short. Proper length of neck must be present for the head to move swiftly.

Body

Powerful, tight and well-balanced. The back, or topline, must be level. The chest is dropped when viewed from the side but actually looks higher when viewed from the front. The loin must be well tucked-up.

Tail

The tail's trunk is thick, the root strong. The Akita must have a curled or wound tail. We cannot stress this enough. The balance, the dignity and the character of the breed depend on the tail's correct carriage. If pulled down the tail should reach the hock.

Anus

Because of the Akita's curled tail, the anus is in an area more visible than on a drop tail breed. It should never

94

protrude, should be fairly large, dark in color and tight.

Legs and Feet

The legs must be muscular, well developed and show power when moving. In the forelegs there must be no hint of the elbows going in or out. In the hindquarters, the hock should turn neither in nor out. The stifle should be only moderately bent.

The feet are large and round. Thick pads and no indication of space between the toes are desired.

Comment

Some words in the American Standard for Akita dogs are: alert, responsive, dignified, courageous, aggressive toward other dogs. Only an Akita with a well wound tail and an alert forward ear set could define these words.

Summary

The Japanese Akita male is a squarely built, powerful, masculine appearing dog. His well-developed, free-of-wrinkle head is full cheeked with a distinct vertical crease running down the center of the forehead. Dark, triangularly shaped eyes complement the small, stand up triangular shaped ears that angle forward. The firmly curled tail is a distinguishing characteristic of the breed. Woolly undercoat, coarse outercoat and harsh, bristled guard hairs protect the body. The stand-off coat is vivid in color and the whiskers are permanent.

The female Akita, although showing like physical characteristics, is slightly longer in body, smaller in size and feminine in appearance and nature.

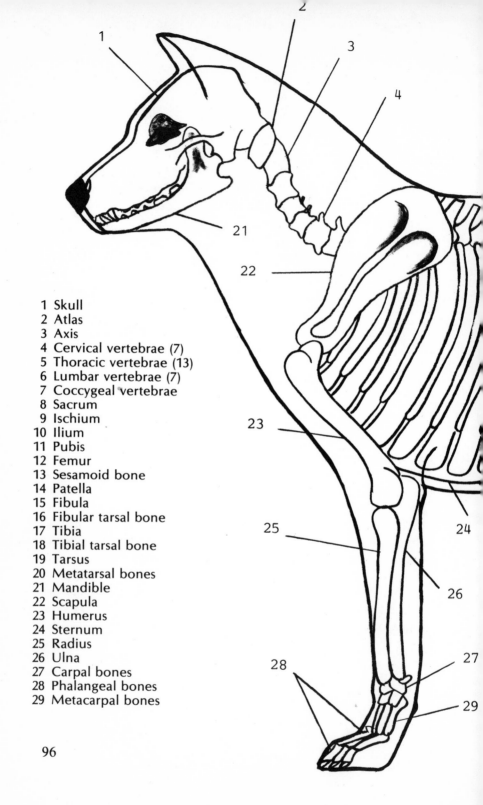

1 Skull
2 Atlas
3 Axis
4 Cervical vertebrae (7)
5 Thoracic vertebrae (13)
6 Lumbar vertebrae (7)
7 Coccygeal vertebrae
8 Sacrum
9 Ischium
10 Ilium
11 Pubis
12 Femur
13 Sesamoid bone
14 Patella
15 Fibula
16 Fibular tarsal bone
17 Tibia
18 Tibial tarsal bone
19 Tarsus
20 Metatarsal bones
21 Mandible
22 Scapula
23 Humerus
24 Sternum
25 Radius
26 Ulna
27 Carpal bones
28 Phalangeal bones
29 Metacarpal bones

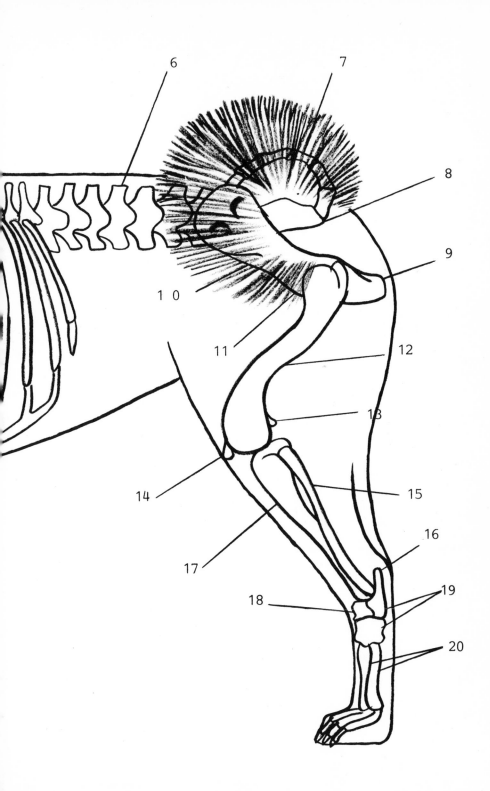

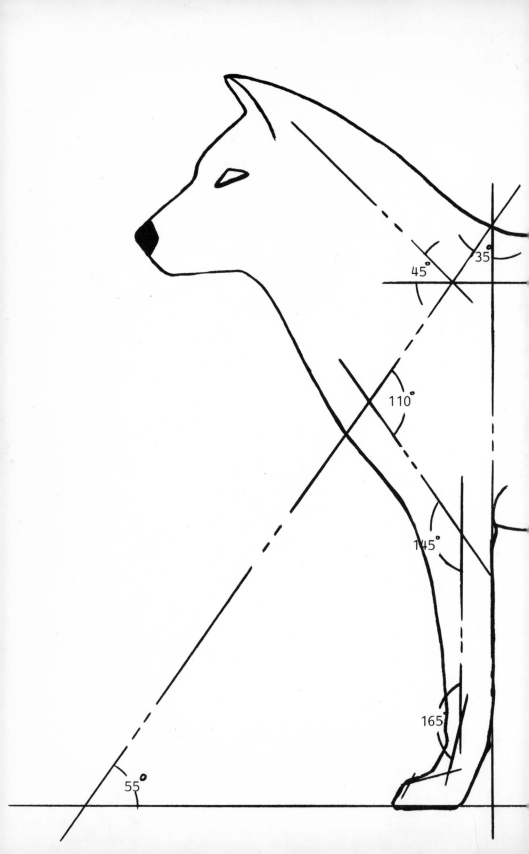

45°

35°

110°

145°

165°

55°

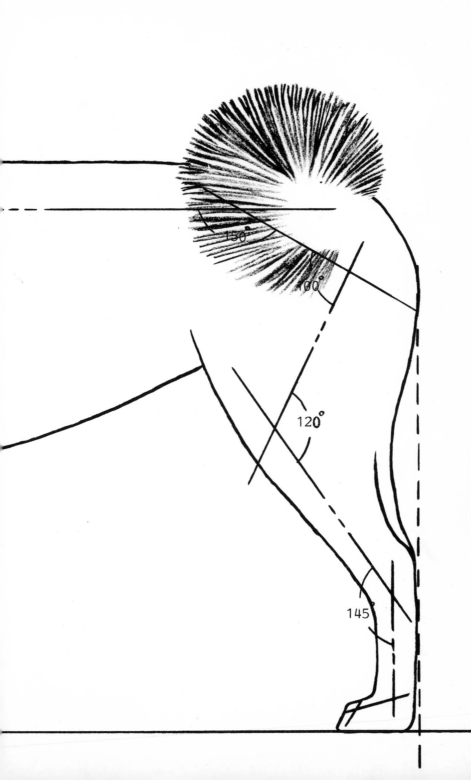

Parts Of The Akita

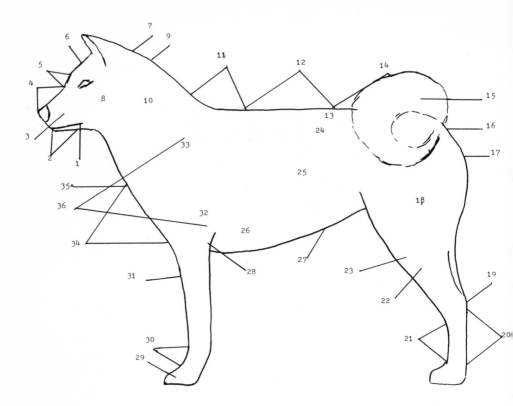

1. flew	14. croup	26. chest
2. lower jaw	15. tail	27. abdomen
3. muzzle	16. tailset	28. elbow
4. foreface	17. point of haunch	29. paws
5. stop	18. thigh	30. pastern
6. skull	19. point of hock	31. forearm
7. occiput	20. hock	32. upper arm
8. cheek	21. metatarsus	33. shoulder blade
9. crest of neck	22. lower thigh	34. fore chest
10. neck	23. point of stifle	35. breast bone or
11. withers	(knee)	prosternum
12. back	24. loin	36. shoulder
13. hip	25. ribs	

7

The Importance of Color

In Japan, in the early days, Japanese dogs were primarily used for hunting and fighting. Performance had priority over color. It was not until the establishment of registration bureaus, whose primary function was and is to preserve the purebreds and strive for ideal standards, that color became a major concern and remains so today.

Because a great percentage of Japan's Akitas are shown and a lesser, but sufficiently large enough number are seen in show rings in the United States, we feel the importance of color warrants a place in this book.

What impact does the show ring have on color?

A dog lacking a vivid and acceptable coat color in Japan very often does not rank high in the show ring, no matter how excellent his facial features, body type or coat quality. Dull, lackluster colors do not do justice to the elegance of the Akita breed, nor do they adhere to the Standard as it is written.

The learned Mr. Naoto Kajiwara, noted Akita authority, in an article on color in the Aiken Journal, Japan, translated by Mr. Tatsuo Kimura, had this to say:

"With the exception of the white coat, the Akita dog's coat color undergoes changes with growth and development. This also adds to the difficulty of judging the true coat color. In the final analysis, one should become capable of judging what he considers to be the appropriate color for each stage of growth. Needless to say, one should consider the color hue admired by the Japanese in the Akita dog that inhabited the Tohoku region from ancient times. That is, color hues that blend with the elegantly pure Japanese paintings, pristine and refined Japanese antique art objects and the simple but sturdy and strong Japanese architecture should be considered. Otherwise, I believe that one could not possibly come to appreciate the feeling for that simplicity without adornment called 'shibusa' or 'soboku' so often expressed by the Japanese."

After World War 2, Pinto, Aka Goma (red sesame), Brindle and Kurogoma (black sesame) were the most popular colors in Japan. Today, reds, good whites and salt and pepper (black and white brindle) are being shown frequently. The Kurogoma color has disappeared, it is said, in order to eliminate such undesirable features as loose skin and wrinkles, for instance, which seemed to go hand in hand with that particular color.

The Pinto or "Buchi" coat pattern varies greatly and is now seen less frequently in Japan than in its heyday of the 1950's. According to Mr. Kajiwara, "Perhaps this may reflect the preference for Akita dogs with the quality of simple dignity without gaudiness."

In the United States, the pintos have never been in heavier demand. Unfortunately, popularity often leads to careless breeding. Because uncaring amateurs forget the Standard for Akita dogs as approved by the A.K.C. which states, "Pinto has a white background with large, *evenly placed patches* covering head and more than one-third of body," freckles, spots, splotches and a lack of pigmentation is being bred into our pintos. "Simple dignity without gaudiness in color" seems to have been forsaken by many breeders in their hurry to fill orders for pinto colored pups.

Fortunately, the other popular Akita coat colors usually do adhere to the Standard.

WHITE: The most desired is a pure white with an almost blueing effect. Dark pigmentation on the eye rims and lips serve as an accent. The nose should be black. Although liver is accepted, the darker the nose the better.

RED: There are many shades of red. The soft coordinating color of the undercoat can change the color of the outer layer. White or black masks are acceptable. The white mask is called hoho-boke (faded cheek color) by the Japanese. When the Akita has tightly drawn black lips, a large black nose and dark eyes of a triangular shape, there is truly nothing more striking or beautiful than the white mask.

BRINDLE: There are various shades of the tiger striped Akita. To quote Mr. Kajiwara, "The pepper and salt brindle has a lighter shade of black, with the muzzle and limbs having a hue as if some frost had descended upon the earth." In the red and black brindle, a strong red is not preferred. Subtlety in color is looked for. A brindle's striping covers the body and may also pattern the face. If the face has stripes instead of a black mask, they should be uniform and not unsightly.

At the Akita Club of America board meeting, February 11, 1972, the color brown was approved as an addition to the list of colors people could use in describing their dogs on the official registration forms. Many people had written to say their Akitas were brown rather than any of the colors mentioned in the registration regulations.

Though the official Standard for Akitas calls for "any color including white," and further states, "Colors are brilliant and clear . . .," we've yet to see a "brilliant and clear" brown. With the exception of the white Akita, most other coat colors become richer and deepen as the the dog matures. The undercoat, on all but the white, is usually a softer shade than the outer layer and the guard hairs. However, it should blend in so there is no evidence of dramatic contrast.

Conclusions

Coat color trends in the breed are often influenced by:

1. A popular stud, prepotent for passing on his color to his winning offspring, e.g., Goromaru-Go (Pinto), Kongo-Go (Kurogoma).

2. Color fads perpetuated by a winning dog who catches the judge's eyes.

3. Personal preference of breeders, the size of their kennels and the number of Akitas produced in relation to kennel size.

Based on the information contained in this chapter, it is suggested breeders put more emphasis on breeding "clear and brilliant" coat colors that are well marked.

Miss Emilie J. Woods, age 4, and companion Ch. Kita Maru, age 12.

Miss Keely Parker, daughter of Mr. and Mrs.
Robert J. Parker II and Teikoku's Hayaku Tezu.

105

8

The Versatility
of the Akita

THE MID-1800's to the early 1920's were rugged times in Japanese society. It was in these years that the early development of the Akita took place.

A toughness and craftiness was instilled in the dog so that he could perform creditably and silently, for these were the rules in those days. At the same time he had to be attractive in appearance for those persons less inclined to violence and more to beauty. Masculine machoism ran rampant and such things as dog baiting and fighting were used to pass time. One can assume, then, that the development of what might have been a more useful and functional breed was arrested by what was bred into it in this era of unrest.

As with any breed, the owners of Akitas tend to put their dogs on a golden pedestal, i.e., "My dog can do no wrong." In truth that pedestal is more often than not slightly tarnished. Although most Akitas have individual endearing qualities, those qualities are for the most part exhibited only to persons closest to them.

In the first years after their introduction to the United States, marvelous words were heard and read. To quote from one early article written on the breed, "The Akita is an intelligent dog, easily trained and handled. A breed of many talents, the Akita is a good working dog who can hunt, retrieve, and track, as well as perform creditably as a seeing eye, rescue, police and guard dog . . ." and on and on until one believed that the Akita was as close to perfection as an animal could be.

Pat Harrington and his family share a laugh with their Akita male.

What the Akita IS, is a most willful opportunist. He is a four-pawed brawling good-sized animal who displays average and sometimes above-average intelligence combined with a cunning not seen in every breed. He manages to endear himself to those who love him, who will exercise control, and who will spend time in an obedience or disciplinary training program with him. A dedicated Akita owner knows this.

Obedience training for the breed was stressed when the first Akitas were brought into the United States but few owners were ready to take on the stubborn nature of the animal.

Ms. Marge Rutherford was one of the first Akita owners to spend time training the breed. She was a trainer for Valley Hills Obedience Club in California and put in many long, dedicated hours in service to the Akita. Ms. Rutherford had a good pair of hands and a gentle, but firm manner. She conducted the first all-Akita breed handling class in 1963.

The first all-Akita obedience trial was held on February 16, 1969 by the Akita Club of America. Homer Wilson judged. Twelve Akitas were entered in Beginning Novice and two in Novice. High Score in Trial went to a bitch, Akita Tani's Kage Boshi, owned by Liz Harrell.

At that same time, an outstanding young brindle male, Mex. Ch. Imperial Rikimaru U.D., owned and trained by Dennis McElrath, was proving that there were exceptions to every rule. Although his sire, Mex. Ch. Kinsei Suna Nihon-No Taishi C.D., had an obedience title, that title was captured only because of the persistence of his owners, Dr. and Mrs. Joseph Vogl. "Tai" was rather slow in the obedience ring; in the breed ring he perked up considerably. His son, "Riki," was just the opposite. He became the first Akita to win a Utility Dog title and was a joy to behold as he worked.

On the East Coast, Sam and Barbara Mullen and Barbara Miller were deeply interested in obedience work and were among the first to enlist the Akita into Brace competition.

In recent years, Midwesterners Dr. Neal Pitts and Sharon Tucker Hansen took top honors with their highly trained dogs. It can be done, but it takes a lot of work and patience.

Kiri Maru on left, working for Marge Rutherford
and the Valley Hills Obedience Club. 1962.

1969 Akita trial showing left to right: Imperial Akiko with Jan Legros, an
unknown Akita with Mr. Roper and Akita Tani's Kagi Boshi with R.C.
Short.

Dr. Joseph Vogl, past president of A.C.A. and Triple "K" Kiyomi C.D.

Mex. Ch. Imperial Rikimaru-Go U.D.

110

Ch. Akita Tani's Yorokobi no Moto C.D.X., T.D., the first Akita to have these titles.

Mr. and Mrs. Michael Barenfeld's Kuro with backpack.

111

Carol Thoene's Shoru-Go, a brindle import who served with the Kern County, California Sheriff's Department in their K-9 unit, was an example of what the properly trained, police trained Akita can do. Few, however, are used for this purpose with success.

When we think of the Akita as a hunting dog, two men come to mind . . . Larry Shepherd who, with his "Shiro," was renowned for the hunting adventures they shared, and Francis Krug. Both men love the outdoors and had infinite patience with their animals.

According to Larry, in his article, "The Akita—Big Game Hunter," April, 1971 issue of *Kennel Review,* "Very few owners have taken their Akitas into the field and conscientiously worked with them to determine their hunting capabilities in this country. We have only scratched the surface in determining their full hunting potential though we have verified he has a hunting background. Any experienced hunter can observe an Akita in the field for ten minutes and conclude that his ancestral lineage was wild and woolly. This conclusion is confirmed by writings telling of his ancestors being scarred by the tusks of wild boar and of their fights with the native Japanese Yezo Bear.

"The Akita has the mental and physical characteristics necessary to be an excellent hunter, combining natural hunting instincts with intelligence. He readily adapts to gunfire; I have heard of few Akitas that are gunshy. His scenting ability compares favorably with many of our sporting breeds and his hearing is better than average. He is a silent hunter and will often adopt a sneak approach when closing in on game he has scented. Though fearless, he advances with caution on game he has sighted and appears to size up his target before attacking. He is tough and strong with a surprising lateral quickness that keeps him out of trouble when confronted by large and dangerous game.

"The Akita has been used with a measure of success as a flusher and is an exceptionally good retriever on land. Though many publicity articles have stated that he is a powerful

Shoru-Go, the police-trained Akita.

swimmer, I have found him to be a poor swimmer in comparison with our well-known water retrievers. His large bone structure and water absorbing coat is not conducive to buoyancy in water. Even so, he will retrieve ducks brought down close to shore.

"He is not a tracker in the hound sense but has been known to follow a blood trail to conclusion. Due to his natural ability and love for hunting, the Akita will do a respectable job on any type of small or medium game but once introduced to big game the adult is separated from the pup.

"Having hunted with many so-called deer dogs, I can state without equivocation that none of those I have seen can compare with the Akita on this type of game. On several occasions my dog has scented and pointed herds of deer between 200 and 300 yards away. On one specific occasion he alerted and followed the scent for a measured 125 yards where he jumped a small bedded-down deer. In one late afternoon and evening hunt, he scented, sighted or jumped nine deer I would never have seen on my own. He is at his best when checking out thickly wooded and brush-covered patches. Working downwind, he will immediately alert if there are deer in these areas.

"As yet, there have been no reports of the Akita being used on wild boar or bear in this country but it is believed to be only a matter of time before their capabilities are recognized and exploited in this field. When this happens, it is my opinion the Akita will turn out to be a surprise package for those taking the time and trouble to do the unwrapping."

Most children who grow up with Akitas learn to control and handle them properly.

Michael and Linda Barenfeld's "Koro" is an Akita of extreme intelligence. He lives high in the Hollywood Hills and looks after his young charge, Adam Barenfeld, with concern. We cannot help but stress once more that toward members of their own family Akitas show an extreme affection, but often with strangers an aloofness prevails. The same reserve exists between two unfamiliar males or two females.

For a personal companion and loving friend the Akita is as pleasurable to have around as any other breed of dog. Once you are willing to accept the fact that the breed as a whole needs extra disciplinary care, training and love, you are in the homestretch. You will have a companion for all seasons.

1978 Grand Champion for weight pulling, Am. Ch. Remwood's Sashi Motto, owned by Mr. and Mrs. William Howard.

Mex. Ch. Kinsei Suna Nihon no Taishi, C.D., guarding his offspring.

Lillian "Papoose" Kletter, a top Junior handler and her Ch. Date Tensha's All About Chesta.

9

Breeding and Whelping
Your Akita Bitch

Y OU'VE REALLY PREPARED for this day. You've
chosen an excellent stud well ahead of time and you're hopeful
the two dogs will complement each other. If you're line
breeding, you've made sure they have common ancestors in the
first three generations.

The breeding contracts have been read, understood, and
signed by both parties. You have kept your bitch in excellent
physical condition. Your veterinarian has checked her, she has
had a laboratory fecal exam, and her immunizations including
Parvovirus have been brought up to date. A vaccination
booster near to time of breeding will give pups greater
immunity against the common puppy diseases. She's had a
pelvic x-ray to determine she is free of hip dysplasia and a
blood test to be sure she doesn't have Brucellosis. You have
also asked for and received proof that the stud is free of hip
dysplasia and his immunizations are up to date.

You took all these precautions because you want your
puppies to be healthy and adhere closely to the standard of
perfection as set down by the American Kennel Club. All in all,
you feel like a Japanese parent who has arranged a marriage.

Your bitch may be ready for breeding as early as the
seventh or eighth day or as late as the 23rd of her estrus. The
average is between the 10th and 14th days. Some bitches are

able to conceive for just a few hours, others have a span of several days. Consecutive vaginal smears taken by your veterinarian several days apart can be used as a guide.

If your bitch is to be shipped to her mate it's important to send her far enough into her heat period so the trip won't stop the season but soon enough to give her time to rest and become acclimated to her surroundings before she is bred. If she is accompanied by someone she knows she will be even more relaxed. But if she must travel alone, insist that the stud's owner or agent have two witnesses verify in writing that a breeding was consummated between your bitch and the stud you selected per the breeding contract.

If you have chosen a local stud, it is wise, on arrival at his kennel, for you and his owner to introduce the two dogs on leads or put them in adjacent pens. A maiden bitch may be frightened if put immediately with a strange stud. There is also a chance she could be an unwilling breeder, in which case there could be quite a row. The bitch is aptly named under certain conditions!

If the two Akitas seem fairly affable release them for courtship. Allow plenty of time, especially if the bitch is new to all of this. When she is ready she will stand for the male and flag her tail to one side. Play it by ear. If she sits down with a puzzled look on her face when her suitor advances, they will both need more than moral support. A gentle assist under the bitch's hindquarters may be all that is required.

Some bitches refuse to be bred even though they are physiologically ready. Although force breeding is not pleasant, it can often be accomplished. It may indeed be the only way to get a recalcitrant bitch bred. Simply muzzle her and hold her still. You might find the "I'd rather do it myself" studs don't always perform under these circumstances.

Mother Nature has a nice process of selective breeding. If not physically or psychologically reproducible then the undesirable trait is not perpetuated in future generations. Let's face it. Not all physically perfect bitches should be bred.

If the mating is successful a "tie" is made between the two

dogs, then the stud dismounts and the two stand on all fours, posterior to posterior until the tie breaks. It is interesting to note the posterior to posterior position dogs assume during mating is an evolutionary selection process. Due to the length of the tie, and being end to end, the so engaged animals were better able to defend themselves from predators. An inexperienced male may need assistance to reach this position. While the two Akitas are tied, both stud and bitch owners should hold their dogs' heads, comfort them if necessary and restrain them from attempting to break away. It is not unusual for the bitch to yelp and whine all through the tie as if she were in mortal agony. Do not despair. No permanent harm is being done. When the tie breaks naturally in anywhere from five to 45 minutes, separate them and offer them a cool drink of water. You may repeat the first breeding in a day or two if the bitch is still receptive. This is an especially good idea if it is stud's first breeding assignment.

From one to three weeks after being bred, a bitch may develop a vaginal infection if dirt was introduced during breeding. Watch for a discharge and make a quick visit to the vet if you see one.

About five weeks after breeding the bitch may appear a little rounded through her hips and abdomen. You may want your veterinarian to verify her pregnancy. He will recommend a vitamin/mineral supplement which you will use regularly throughout the pregnancy. The bitch's appetite may increase by the fifth week. This is the time to add to her food intake. The meals should have the correct amount of protein and calcium per body weight. Because of space taken up by the growing pups, meals broken into twice-a-day feedings are recommended. Remember a fat bitch does not whelp easily as a general rule so don't stuff your Akita indiscriminately. Exercise regularly, in moderation, to keep trim.

Water must always be available. It helps prevent constipation and maintain good health. Do not try any home remedies. Many such medicines designed for humans can be lethal for dogs. And be on guard against well-meaning friends who have a cure for anything that may go wrong with your bitch. Listen politely, thank them for their advice, then call your veterinarian to learn what to do.

Exercise is important to maintain muscle tone and to aid in a speedy and easy whelping. Violent exercise and jumping are to be avoided. As the bitch becomes heavier she will most likely limit her actions. Many bitches who used to be the first one in on a family wrestle now will sit sedately on the sidelines.

Everyday grooming is a good idea. Not only will it keep the mother-to-be's skin in good condition and her coat clean, she will have that little bit of extra attention so vital while in the "family way." Should some unforeseen skin infection or other ailment arise, you will discover it quickly in a daily grooming session.

Toward the end of the pregnancy, keep your bitch's belly clean by bathing it with bland soap. The hair surrounding the nipples will gradually begin to fall out, preparing her body for the coming event.

The Whelping Box

The most important piece of equipment to have in readiness for the big event is the whelping box or pen. Made of plywood, it should be large enough for the bitch to stretch out in all directions when she is nursing, with room left over for the pups to move around in as they mature. One and one-half times the length of the bitch is a good rule of thumb. If it is too big, puppies can wander away from the warmth of the nest and unduly exasperate the new mother.

The sides should be high enough to keep the pups in but low enough to let Mom out easily. Four inches up from the flooring, a one by four-inch smooth wooden board should be attached to the sides with small angle irons, all around as a rail. This will prevent the bitch from accidentally smothering to death any puppy which crawls behind her. You might also consider raising your box a few inches off the floor, especially if it's on a concrete floor or you live in a cold climate. If your box

119

is not raised, do put a layer of heavy construction-type plastic under it to prevent dampness.

After you have made your box, layer its floor with a generous padding of newspaper. It is easier to peel off soiled sheets of paper during and after whelping than it is to move mother and babies from one corner to the next while you lay new paper.

As the whelping box is being constructed, your bitch will show no interest. She may go about digging holes in the yard, her own way of preparing her nest. The box should, for this reason, be constructed and in place at least two weeks in advance of whelping so that she can be encouraged to sleep in it. If she has a favorite rug or toy, place it in the pen to help her understand that she is to nest there instead of under the house!

The Outside Pen

Another, but not immediate need, is an outside pen. This should be mobile. A discarded baby playpen is often useful for this purpose. Sunshine and fresh air promote healthy pups; the outside pen can be put into use when the pups are about three weeks old.

Some precautions should be noted:

a) If you are going to use an old-fashioned playpen with wood slats, cover the entire outside with small-holed wire mesh, making sure the nails or brads attaching it to the slats do not protrude inside. Not only will this type of covering prevent the pups from escaping when they are tiny, they will be unable to get stuck between the rails when they are bigger.

b) The pen must be situated so the pups have both sunshine and shade at all times and not be in drafty areas.

c) The pups should never be left alone in the pen when you are away from the house, even for a few minutes. There are too many interested people with poor intentions in this world.

The First-Aid Kit

Last but not least is the first-aid kit. Some items

Vera Bohac's Sakura and her puppies.

Brandy presents Terry Caudill with a litter.

Long hair or "Moku" Akita puppy. A
good example of an undesirable trait.

mentioned here may not be used by everyone but it is wise to have most of these on hand:

1. Box lined with towels for the pups.
2. Heating pad or hot water bottle to keep pup box warm.
3. Pile of clean terrycloth towels to dry the pups.
4. Stack of newspapers. (You will need every paper you can lay your hands on. Ask everyone you know to save theirs for you. Don't wait until the last minute. It is unbelievable how fast they will be used up!)
5. Vaseline.
6. Rubber gloves.
7. Soap.
8. Iodine to sterilize ends of umbilical cords.
9. Blunt scissors to cut umbilical cords.
10. Alcohol to keep scissors sterilized.
11. Rectal thermometer.
12. White thread to tie off umbilical cords.
13. Flashlight.
14. Waste container.
15. Baby scale to weigh each pup at birth.
16. Clock.
17. Sleeping bag or cot (for you).
18. Pencil and paper to record whelping details. The memory alone is not a reliable source. Write everything down. Any unusual detail of labor, the length of the labor, the birth time of each pup and each pup's description including weight at birth.
19. Soft tissues to use in absorbing mucus from nose and mouth.

The Whelping

Puppies are normally born between the 58th and 63rd day after breeding. One sign of impending motherhood is when the bitch's temperature falls from her average 100.5-101.5 degrees F. to about 97 degrees F. A dip in temperature for any length of time could mean whelping is about to begin. It may be a matter of hours or a couple of days, but it *is* an encouraging sign.

How do you take a dog's temperature? Have the bitch stand up or lie on one side. Lubricate the rectal thermometer with vaseline and insert into the rectum 1½ inches or so. Hold your fingers close to the thermometer just in case the bitch moves suddenly. Talk to her to soothe her. IMPORTANT: Never leave her for a moment while the thermometer is inserted. Let that phone ring. If a family crisis occurs, start again later but NEVER LEAVE HER!

Three minutes after insertion is ample time for an accurate reading, but we do suggest you take the temperature a couple of times a day and at the same time every day, preferably not after eating or exercising.

Restlessness is another sign that whelping will soon begin. Pamper your bitch and remain calm. You are her steadying force. She will dig holes and pace. She is reacting to her most basic instincts. Encourage her to use the whelping box.

Speaking of basic instincts, the whelping area will probably be more acceptable if it is removed from the mainstream of family traffic and, if possible, dimly lighted. Wild dogs prefer caves and holes. Although you may not like to think of your sweet *Mesu,* the Japanese word for female dog, as basically wild, a deep-seated instinct to nest as her ancestors did is still very much there. So help her to satisfy her needs where you can.

When one or both of the aforementioned signs of whelping shows, turn your attention to the whelping area itself. Temperature should be between 85 and 80 degrees F. for the first two weeks of the pups' lives. Be alert for drafts and dampness. Additional heat in the form of an electric heater may be used *near* the pen, never directly over it. Put a thermometer at floor level of the pen (not in it) so there will be no question of temperature. Some breeders use a heat lamp over the pen. We suggest you discuss this with your veterinarian.

Where and when the bitch first strains and has her first pup can be a wonder. Rarely will she pick a time when it is light out and the dishes are washed! Rather it will probably be soon after you have settled in for the night. So grab your kerchief and coat or robe and help her out. Lists and precautions, rules and regulations whiz through your head. In the long run Mother Nature and common sense win out most of the time. Your flighty little female suddenly becomes the most matronly of matrons, tossing away those carefree days of irresponsibility and settling into her nest to whelp her young. Hopefully, she has picked the whelping box and not a mud puddle in the middle of a thunderstorm!

Speaking of mudpuddles, a word to the wise. If you are taking your bitch out to relieve herself either just before whelping or mid-whelping, take along another person, a pair of scissors, a towel and if it is nighttime, a flashlight. She may decide your flower bed is a romantic place to relieve herself . . . of a puppy. If she does, you are prepared.

Whelping time is most unpredictable and depends on litter size, age and experience of bitch, mothering instincts, etc. During the first stage of labor the passages are stretching and softening. Very often the bitch will pace. She may even yelp or whimper once in a while. She may rip apart every paper in her carefully prepared whelping box and wash herself so frequently you are sure the skin will wear off.

During the second stage of labor, she is content to lie down and is happy to have you with her. Warning: Do not ask your neighbors to come and watch. You do not want the bitch to become apprehensive. Only members of the immediate family should be allowed to stay, provided they remain quiet and calm. Use your own discretion about children. The mother will probably be breathing deeply now and will clench her paws as contractions begin. She will be panting in between.

125

As the contractions become stronger, the panting becomes steady. The eyes may become slightly glazed. Then, miracle of miracles, a watery fluid seeps from the vulva, sometimes with a soft popping noise. The tail arches and with one or more contractions, a pup arrives. An especially large pup may cause the bitch to strain a bit more before delivery.

Puppies can be born head first or hind-end first (breech). Both positions are normal.

Most Akita bitches are quite capable of taking care of every detail of the whelping. Some are even awed by it all. These consider themselves fascinated observers as the first couple of pups present themselves. You can help here and later on if your new mother should tire.

Each pup is born in a membraneous sac of water. An umbilical cord leads from the sac to the placenta. If the bitch fails to clean the membrane off the pup's head immediately, you must, so the pup can start breathing. You may insert your finger in the pup's mouth with absorbent tissue to clear the breathing passages if it is necessary.

If the bitch does not cut the cord, let the pup lie for a moment while the blood in the cord flows into him, then tie the cord in two places with thread. Using sterile scissors, cut between the two ties, about two inches from the pup's abdomen, and daub the end with iodine.

As each membrane is removed and the cry of life is given, your heart skips a beat and perhaps a tear of emotion runs down your cheek. But while it is a time for reverence, it is also a time for action. Keep two things in mind: newborn pups need warmth and fluids. If the mother does not start licking the pup to dry and stimulate it, your handy stack of towels comes into action. Check the mouth and nostrils to make sure they are clear. Rub the pup until it is dry and warm.

After each puppy comes the spongy placenta or afterbirth which your bitch may consume even before she cares for the pup. Don't worry. This is a natural instinct. In the wild, the afterbirths served as the bitch's only source of food for several days while she looked after her newly whelped litter.

It is imperative you check for each afterbirth. It is vital they all be expelled. If they are not, the bitch could get a uterine infection which can endanger her life and that of her litter. These suggestions are not made to scare you. They are given for your peace of mind so that you can enjoy this whole, marvelous experience free of worry.

Each pup is born with a waxy plug, Meconium, about one inch long, in its large intestine. The licking action of the mother should bring this plug out of the rectum soon after birth. If Mom seems slack you can help by stroking the pup's stomach. When about one-half of the plug appears, take hold and pull it gently, straight out.

The pups must have a chance to nurse for their fluid and be kept warm while their brothers and sisters are whelped. Your veterinarian can help here. There are several methods of keeping the pups warm. One general rule, however, is to always keep the pups near the bitch's head so she can see them and tend to them.

The colostrum, or first milk the puppies drink, is important to their health. It is high in vitamins A and D and carries with it antibodies against diseases for which the bitch has been immunized. It is also laxative and helps get the pups' little bodies to function normally.

If you should have a pup that is having difficulty in breathing, hold it firmly in a towel, head away from you and swoop it in a head to knee movement. You are trying to empty the liquid from the nostrils and mouth. Do this several times, making sure to support the head and neck with the pup lying on its back.

Between puppies, do put the delivered babies on the milk "faucets." This makes the bitch relax and feel secure. When it looks like another puppy is on the way, remove the delivered ones to their warm box near the bitch's head.

After a long time with no straining or panting and no puppies, the whelping could be over but the bitch will need the veterinarian's attention to make sure. He will most likely give her an injection to make the uterus contract and rid it of any

127

fluids and retained afterbirth material. Pituitrin also stimulates the flow of milk. Normally, full lactation occurs in three days. Your veterinarian also may want to give the new mother an antibiotic to insure against uterine infection, and, of course, go over the new litter to see they are healthy.

Conclusions

You should let your veterinarian know ahead of time the approximate dates the pups are expected. Advise him when the bitch actually goes into active labor so that he will be available should you need him.

Be sure to ask him what to do if a pup is born seemingly lifeless. And, how to help if a pup, though being born normally, gets stuck in the birth canal. Do not confuse this with a pup who may be positioned incorrectly in the birth canal. This is a job for the veterinarian. Never try to reach into the birth canal, for any reason.

Now that you have seen your bitch through a normal birth you should be aware of signs to look for in an abnormal one. Call your veterinarian if the bitch is:

1. Having visible contractions more than two hours before producing a pup.

2. In excessive pain.

3. Doing excessive straining.

4. Trembling, shivering, with cold extremities.

5. In collapse and exhaustion.

6. Vomiting.

7. Depressed after starting labor.

Billy O'Shea and friends.

Shinbei with Twyla Lusk.

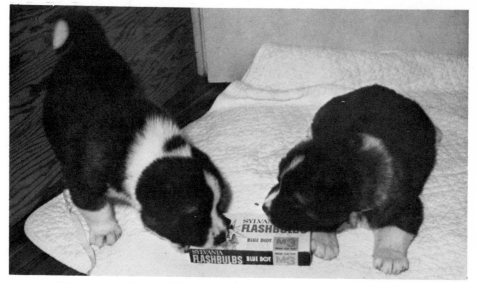

Youngsters from Oshio Kennel, Long Beach, California.

129

10

Your New Akita Litter

After the Whelping

Now that the whelping is over and mother and babies are doing well, check the room temperature and offer the bitch water and some soft food.

Look in on the happy family often during the first few hours. This is a pleasurable task and important. Tiny as they are, puppies can wriggle away from the group and become chilled. There are always those strong puppies who dominate the milk bar and take away from the smaller or weaker pups. It's up to you to see that everyone has an equal chance.

Do not hesitate to handle the pups. They need to know the warmth of kind human hands right from the start. Always hold them gently but securely. Hold them close to the mother's face so she will not become anxious. Teach your children how to hold them when the pups are older. Have them sit on the floor of the pen so there is no chance of a pup being dropped. Only do this if you have a bitch who is agreeable to it.

Be thoughtful of your bitch and don't bring the neighbors in to view the litter for at least three to four weeks. When you do invite them in, bring only one or two people at a time. Ask them to be quiet and stand at a distance. It's wise to have as first visitors persons the bitch knows well and likes. It's also best to eliminate those who own dogs. They could transmit disease to your pups. Precautions like these will help keep your mortality rate low.

The pups' basic needs for warmth and fluids will be met by the mother entirely for the first two weeks. After two weeks most pups can stand air temperature of about 70° F. Dampness and drafts are still to be avoided. A hand on a huddle of puppies should feel pleasantly warm. It is just as cruel to keep the pups in overheated conditions as to keep them cold. The room temperature at pen level should be your ever constant guideline.

Until the umbilical cords have dried up, check them daily and apply iodine to the ends to aid in drying and prevent infection.

When the bitch is nursing her diet will have to increase in respect to the pups' growths and demands for milk. Sometimes the bitch needs many times her normal amount. Therefore, it is wise to feed her several times a day. Her diet must have sufficient milk, meat, fat, fortified kibble and the vitamin supplement prescribed by your veterinarian. For the first few days she may be reluctant to leave her pups even for a few minutes. Feed her in the pen, lying down if she prefers. Pamper her. She deserves it.

There Are Pitfalls

Now that you have found happiness in your warm puppies, we will warn you of some pitfalls. Rarely does everything go smoothly. Be prepared for the problems that could crop up.

Often, for some reason, puppies fade away. Just as simple as that. Instead of gaining weight they lose. This happens quickly. Unless you have baby scales and keep daily weight records, you have lost a puppy or more before you realize what is happening. A slight weight drop in the first day or two is not abnormal.

One to three ounces of weight gain per day is fairly average for an Akita puppy. If your pups are not gaining at this rate, perhaps they're not getting enough mother's milk.

Tenseness. Nerves. Diet. One of these might dry up the

131

mother's milk. If you think it is needed, supplement, using a small baby bottle filled with formula for puppies. There are several excellent formulas on the market, one of which your vet may recommend. Two other formulas that have been used with success by breeders are:

1 cup milk			1 cup milk
		or	1 egg yolk
3 raw eggs			1 tsp. corn oil
			1 tsp. Karo Syrup
			1 tsp. limewater

Every eight hours give about 1.5 ounces of formula per ten ounces of puppy weight. You must stroke the puppy's genitals with a piece of cotton moistened with warm water to relieve it after feeding.

Instead of using the baby bottle to supplement, many breeders tube-feed. If your vet suggests this method, be sure you know how to use it. Don't attempt it without his demonstrating it to you first. Use the tube only if a pup is too weak to bottle-feed.

Viral infections and bacterial disease are more common than is usually realized, and are also a reason puppies fade. Frequent sterilization of feeding utensils is imperative. Milk is a breeding ground for bacteria. According to *The Complete Dog Book*—The American Kennel Club, mortality of young puppies may be as high as 20% to 30% per litter. This doesn't mean you will lose this many, but if you own a large kennel, that is what you could expect over a period of time.

Watch your bitch carefully during the heavy nursing period, especially if she has a large litter. Eclampsia, a metabolic disorder involving the blood calcium level, may occur in nursing bitches or bitches in late pregnancy. Several cases have been reported in the Akita breed. The first indication is extreme nervousness and rapid breathing. If she is not treated at once, the bitch will develop a stiff gait and seem to be under the influence of a martini or two. Within a short time she will fall and be rigid in appearance with intermittent severe muscle spasms. Then follows a period of convulsions which could lead to death.

Treatment should be immediate, at the first signs of the condition. You can buy time by giving your bitch one adult size, 5-grain aspirin tablet per 10 pounds of body weight. The chemical action produced by the aspirin will cause a rapid rise in the bloodstream's calcium level, but only temporarily. A veterinarian should be consulted immediately for intravenous calcium and supportive treatment.

Further nursing of this bitch is to be discouraged. You will have to hand nurse the litter. Rig up a loose bandage type of cover for the bitch's breasts, so that when she is returned to the litter the pups will not nurse.

Painful swelling or congestion of the breasts can be relieved by allowing the puppies to nurse two or three times daily for 10 to 15 minutes each time. Camphorated oil, massaged into the breasts, will also help relieve the condition.

In most cases, eclampsia can be avoided by using a well balanced diet throughout the pregnancy. Prenatal vitamin mineral supplement from the time of breeding through weaning is a must.

A puppy that appears to be in pain, struggling to relieve itself, may have impacted bowels. This condition has happened in puppies from something as simple as swallowing sand or pea gravel. A mild laxative or suppository recommended by your vet can relieve the situation that is causing the pup so much discomfort.

Weaning, Worming and Care

All changes in feeding your puppies should be made gradually. At two to three weeks of age, they are ready to be trained to pan feeding. This is merely a supplementation of their diet with solid food. Pablum or a good baby cereal mixed with one of the above-mentioned formulas is a good starter. Hamburger and cottage cheese can be gradually added to the above. This should be fed four times a day for three to four weeks. Little by little the pups will be completely weaned.

Nan Chao's Fox of Hidden Acres and owner Sue Sanett.

Seven week old littermates.

135

Start adding the commercial dog food you intend to use in the future, a little at a time. Increase as the pups mature. Do be careful not to get them too heavy. More harm than good can come from overfeeding. The fat, chubby puppy of today is not the healthy dog of tomorrow. Overweight can result in structural breakdown. Consultation with your veterinarian can help you provide the correct vitamin and mineral supplements if they are needed.

Let us assume your bitch was wormed prior to conception and considered to be worm-free at the time of the puppies' birth. You still owe it to the buyers of your puppies to make sure roundworms or some other form of parasite are not present. At approximately five weeks of age, take a stool sample from each pup to your vet. If he detects parasites, he will either prescribe medicine or have you bring the pups in so he can clean them out. It's a good idea to get a certificate stating either that the pups are free of parasites, or the date of worming if it took place. Every six months is a good rule of thumb for taking in stool samples throughout a dog's life.

The most enjoyable part of raising puppies is watching them grow and develop. Try not to get too attached to any one pup and neglect the others. Give all of them the attention and human companionship they need at this crucial period of development. Try to spend at least 15 minutes a day with each one, apart from the litter. Begin leash-breaking between six and seven weeks of age for short periods of time.

Make it a point each day to clean the whelping box and its tenants. Then spend some time grooming the bitch and wiping off the puppies if they look as if they could use it. By doing this on a daily basis, mother and her brood will feel secure. Eventually the wiping can turn into brushing, clipping the little nails, and, in general, preparing them for grooming in their adult lives. For nails, use a pair of blunt-edged manicuring scissors, the kind sold for babies, as insurance against injury to bitch and each other.

Cleaning the whelping box is quite simple if you own three sections of indoor-outdoor carpeting the size of the box.

136

Carpet can be hosed off and dries quickly. Most important, it provides a good surface for the pups to walk on. It's not slippery like newspapers. Consideration should be given to replacing the newspapers with the carpet or a non-skid material a day or two after whelping.

The Fine Art of Culling

To cull a litter is to make sure that its worse members do not repeat their faults in progeny of their own. There are many reasons to consider culling. We must assume that every person who breeds an Akita bitch or dog is interested in improving the quality of the breed as a whole. As an individual concerned with the betterment of your breed, you must bear in mind what you would do if the following occurred:

A litter of seven puppies blessed your home. Two were marked much like Dalmatians. One had an abundance of coat. One had a narrow pin head. The rest seemed to be lovely pups.

You may decide to wait and see what they look like when they are eight to ten weeks old. During this time it is not fair to the public or the breed to put this litter on the selling block. If, at the end of your waiting period, some of the pups are not what you would want seen in the show ring, much less bred, it's up to you to do what will benefit the breed.

There are two ways of culling. Obviously defective pups may be put to sleep painlessly by a veterinarian shortly after birth. Or, strictly pet caliber animals may be placed in loving homes with a written contract guaranteeing they will be spayed or castrated before they reach breeding age.

Culling is a touchy subject but when you are striving for perfection for your breed, and when you realize that the world is already overcrowded with people and animals, there is a lot to be said in its defense.

Registration and Sale of Puppies

Now comes paperwork and heartbreak time. First the paperwork. Register your litter with the American Kennel

Ch. Sakusaku's Domino-Go at three months. When he matured he was first Group placing Akita in Hawaii. Owner, Richard Kawamoto.

Camille Kam and R. H. K.'s Musumo-Go in Hawaii. Owner, Richard Kawamoto.

Club and prepare the individual forms they send you for the new owners.

If there are puppies you feel should not be individually registered (refer to section on culling), make sure your contract of sale includes this provision. In other words, have total agreement with your puppy buyers on the status of their new puppies, in writing, at time of sale.

Along with the registration papers, give each new owner a sales receipt, a health record, a diet and a contract detailing provisions of registration and/or sterilization agreements. A manual for new puppy owners is also a good idea.

Most important is a *correct* pedigree. It has come to our attention that some persons have received pedigrees containing incorrect spelling of dogs' names *and,* in some instances, the wrong ancestors. A pedigree is like a birth certificate and should be treated as such. The names *must* be correct. There is no room for error in making them out.

The best interests of the breed and the public should take precedence over monetary gain to the breeder. Price your litter fairly, according to individual evaluation and be consistent with the going rate of other purebred dogs of equal merit. It's important to remember that when you set a high value on a pup and predict a glorious future for it. the buyer will usually hold you to the outcome you predict. For this reason it's wise to say to him about the pup he selects, "He has show potential . . . now."

As any good breeder will tell you, determining a puppy's future ring status at age eight or ten weeks is a difficult thing to do.

After all of your wee prides and prejudices have left the nest, you must think of getting mama's girlish figure back. While you can't ship her off to a health spa, you can cut back on her food intake. Make sure she has a balanced diet, plenty of exercise and keep her well-groomed.

Within four months, with careful treatment, your Akita bitch can once again be the household treasure.

11

American Breed Clubs

The Akita Club of America

The Akita Club of America is the parent club. "The Early History of the Akita in America" covers its formative years.

In 1962, the club welcomed the Imperial Akita Club of Southern California into its fold as its first franchised chapter. Unfortunately, it was short-lived. The Eastern Akita Club, formed in 1963, was A.C.A.'s second chapter and remained intact until recognition of the breed.

In June, 1964, the parent club presented more than 400 registrations, a Stud Book and assorted other documents to the American Kennel Club in a bid for recognition but A.K.C. felt the time was not right for recognition and sent all records back to California.

Five years later A.C.A. sponsored a symposium at the Anaheim Convention Center in Southern California. Dr. Frederick Pitts served as moderator. Joan Linderman was co-coordinator. A growing sophistication and thirst for knowledge among members drew a large audience. Club statistics showed that seven generations of Akitas had been bred in the United States. In 1969, 242 individual applications had been received for registration. That same year saw the founding of the Akita Rescue League whose function it was to aid homeless Akitas. All chapters of the parent club were

The new Akiho Headquarters in Japan 1980.

Karafuta dog statues at the base of the Tokyo
Tower building. *Photo by G. Linderman*

Akita Statuary.

Inside AKIHO'S record vault. A small section.

Equipment and shoes used by the early Matagi hunters. Akita museum in Odate.

Dog statue in the Akita museum at AKIHO headquarters.

involved in an X-Ray Certification Program for hip dysplasia. From this point on the quest for recognition became an obsession with most parent club members.

The United States is divided into five regions by the parent club. Each region elects one representative to sit as a voting member on the Akita Club of America Board of Directors. Within these geographical regions are individual clubs, some of which are member clubs of the Akita Club of America. Member clubs have no direct connection with the regional representatives.

Regions

Northeastern, Region 1: Maine, New Hampshire, Vermont, Massachusetts, Rhode Island, Connecticut, New Jersey, New York, Pennsylvania, Ohio.

Southeastern & Southern, Region 2: Delaware, Maryland, Virginia, West Virginia, North Carolina, South Carolina, Georgia, Florida, Alabama, Tennessee, Kentucky, Mississippi, Missouri, Arkansas, Louisiana, Oklahoma, Texas.

North and South Central, Region 3: Indiana, Illinois, Michigan, Wisconsin, Iowa, North Dakota, South Dakota, Nebraska, Kansas, Montana, Wyoming, Colorado, New Mexico, Idaho, Utah, Arizona, Minnesota.

Western, Region 4: Alaska, Washington, Oregon, Nevada, Hawaii, Northern California (above a line parallel with Bakersfield).

Southern California, Region 5: All of California below a line parallel with the northern city limits of Bakersfield).

Member Clubs

Akita Club of Delaware Valley
New Jersey

Akita Club of Tampa Bay
Florida

Great Lakes Akita Club
Illinois

Akita Club of Las Vegas
Nevada

144

Buckeye Akita Club Ohio	Kin Ken Akita Club of Southern California
Akita Club of Long Island New York	Cascade Akita Club Oregon
Rocky Mountain Akita Club Colorado	Akita Club of Puget Sound Washington
Colonial Akita Club Maryland	Squakheag Akita Club Connecticut

Akitainu Hozonkai

The Nisei week Akita show held in August, 1969, spurred much interest among Akita fanciers in the Los Angeles area. With encouragement from Akiho, Japanese judge, Dr. K. Ogasawara, and permission and aid from Japan, the only branch of Akitainu Hozonkai outside Japan was formed in Los Angeles, California.

First Branch Chairman was Walter Imai. His and his official staff's contribution to the Akita breed was monumental. Their bulletins carried translations of historical documents as well as standards and articles on the breed as they were received from Japan. Akiho meetings were well attended. Photos, movies and slides illustrated the breed in Japan. A highlight in the lives of Akiho Branch members occurred some years ago when Kusumaru, a Tokuyu winner, a dog designated as "Superior" in Japan, was presented to Walter Imai by Mr. and Mrs. Taro Matsuda, owners of one of the most prominent Akita kennels in Tokyo, Japan. Joan and Jerry Linderman had the privilege of visiting the Matsudas in their lovely home in Japan. Their hospitality was typical of the good will shown by all Akita people in that country.

Since 1970, the Nisei week Akiho show has been sponsored by the parent Akiho club who provides the judge for each one of these events. He not only judges the dogs but holds seminars which are a source of enrichment for fanciers starved for truthful information about their breed.

It is felt that the Los Angeles Branch had its greatest moment when they shared the dedication of the new Akiho Headquarters in Odate, Japan with the parent club.

The building is truly a monument to the breed. Costing over $400,000 to erect, it is supported by its nearly 60 branch clubs. From the gigantic mosaic of Akita dogs in the lobby to the spacious conference rooms, a huge walk-in vault for registrations and historical documents, to the third floor museum that depicts the evolution and history of the Akita breed, it is a masterpiece of design.

At this writing, we are now into 1982. Akiho, Los Angeles Branch still disseminates information, still holds its annual show and is still a credit to the Akita breed. Those of us who believe that a perfect or near-perfect Akita lies cradled in the Orient fervently hope this link with the breed will flourish and be an aid in opening the doors to much needed imports who can only benefit our beloved Akita dog.

Ch. Gin-Gin Haiyaku-Go of Sakusaku. The first Best in Show Akita in Canada, "Chester" was owned by S. Kletter. *Ludwig*

Ch. Checan's Subarashii Checan, winner of the first Canadian Booster Show. Owners, Dr. and Mrs. George Bohac.

12

The Akita in Canada

Even though the Akita's history dates back centuries, its appearance in Canada is quite recent.

In the late 1950's, the Akitas to step foot on Canadian soil were brought into Smithers, north central British Columbia; a male by Dr. Jim Proctor, and a female by Mr. Ed Carder.

Jerry and Sheryl Langan bought their first Akita from the first litter, whelped in 1960, out of this pair. In February, 1969, the Langans brought in Akita Tani's Empress Akiko, from California.

Sonia Sitz and Kaye Otsuka came into contact with some American breeders and purchased the male puppy, Nikko No Nikka Yuken. Gary and Joy Kennedy were next to purchase a female pup from the States. It would be correct to say that the evolution of the Akita breed in Canada began in the West.

According to Vera Bohac, former President of the Akita Club of Canada, "To the best of my knowledge, the first Akitas in Eastern Canada were those of Dr. Ted Thomas during the early 1970's. Shortly thereafter, Dr. Gary Seawright brought his Akitas in from the United States, and jointly, with Dr. Thomas, began breeding them."

Several of Canada's early Akitas were registered with the Akita Club of America but were not recognized by the American Kennel Club or the Canadian Kennel Club so they could not be shown in the official classes and could not be registered.

A common goal, then, brought the first Akita owners together to form a club. In April, 1972, in Lethbridge, Alberta at an historic meeting, Sonia Sitz, Kaye Otsuka and Gary and Joy Kennedy formed the Akita Club of Canada. Several months of hard work produced a constitution and by-laws and in October, 1972, the club was recognized by the Canadian Kennel Club. To achieve recognition of the breed, two major requirements had to be fulfilled: the Breed Standard and 25 specimens of the breed, not to mention some other formalities.

Akitas made their first unofficial appearance in show rings in Canada in June 1972 when the first Akita with a transit pass was shown at the Calgary Kennel Club show. It was Sonia Sitz's male, Nikko No Nikka Yuken.

In January 1973 Akitas were able to compete in the Miscellaneous Class. A month later, two Akitas were shown at the Alberta Kennel Club show in Calgary. They were Nikka and the Kennedys' female, Kyoko. The dogs were introduced to then President of Canadian Kennel Club, Mrs. Hilda Pugh, to the Canadian Kennel Club Representative, and to the public.

In July, 1973, Sheryl Langan's Tani's Empress Akiko won first in Miscellaneous Class and Best of Breed at Prince George, B.C. In that same month, at Millarville, Alberta, Dianne Wagner's Akita Tani's Kita placed third in Miscellaneous Class.

The Stud Book was set up in duplicate by Mrs. Kaye Otsuka and submitted to Canadian Kennel Club in August, 1974. The Breed Standard was written and finally, the magic number of 25 dogs was reached. With pleasure, Sonia Sitz announced in the October, 1974 issue of *TA YORI,* the official publication of the Akita Club of Canada, as unofficial news from Canadian Kennel Club, that the Akita would be recognized as of January 1, 1975 and that the accepted standard for this newly recognized breed would be published in the November, 1974 issue of *Dogs in Canada* magazine. It was a dream come true. The original creators of the club, headed by Sonia Sitz, deserve full credit for the recognition of the Akita

149

breed in Canada.

After breed recognition, the first Akitas to be shown in official classes were in Calgary, in January, 1975. They were three littermates from the first Canadian registered litter produced by Dianne Wagner, Daiken Akitas. Shortly thereafter, in March, 1975, the first Canadian Champion Akita was named. It was Kenjiko Royal Tenji. Vera Bohac's female Akita, Daiken No Sakura became the first female Canadian born Champion in June, 1975.

As the breed grew and its popularity thrived in Canada, the club also grew. With this growth came the inevitable problems which often accompany changes. These problems were gradually settled and a new step in the club's evolution began. The club, which once centered in Western Canada, has now spread over the whole nation. Representatives were appointed for each province and became liaisons between the club officials and members all over the country. The official newsletter *Tayori* was upgraded and now serves as the main communication within the club. It is in this way the members are kept informed and involved in club activities.

During 1977, the Akita Club of Canada organized the first Canadian Akita booster show which was held in Lethbridge, Alberta on April 16th. Ch. Checan's Subarashii Checan, owned by Vera Bohac, was the winner. The same year also saw the first Akita go Best in Show. Ch. Gin Gin Haiyaku-Go of Sakusaku C.A.C.I.B. garnered the award at the St. Francis Kennel Club Show, Bromont, Quebec on July 1st, under Judge Mr. J. Stanek. Canadian born Ch. Langan's Amaterasu O-Mi-Kami, owned by Andy and Dani Russell, was the first Best Puppy in Show Akita in Canada. The first obedience title was received by Daiken's Kuro Kuma, C.D., co-owned by Constable Barry Bell and Dianne Wagner.

The Akita Club of Canada's standing objectives are to protect and promote the breed, prevent cross-breedings, provide information, knowledge and education, so that the public may come to know this wonderful breed as a loyal friend of man.

150

The Revised Standard for the Akita Breed as Approved at the February 19th, 1975 Meeting of The Board of Directors of The Canadian Kennel Club

1. *Origin and Purpose:*

The Akita, whose history dates back some 300 years, derives its name from the Prefecture of Akita, in northern Japan. At one time, in the early days of the breed, Akitas were considered a national treasure and only nobles could own one. In 1931, this beautiful dog was proclaimed a natural monument by the Japanese Ministry of Education, and the government took all necessary steps to preserve the breed. The Akita is primarily a working dog and has been used for guard work, a guide for the blind, a protector of children and home, a hunting companion and sled work.

2. *General Appearance:*

Large, powerful, alert, with much substance and heavy bone, the broad head, forming a blunt triangle, with deep muzzle, small eyes and erect ears carried forward in line with back of neck, is characteristic of the breed. The large, curled tail, balancing the broad head, is also a characteristic of the breed.

3. *Temperament:*

Alert and responsive, dignified and reserved but courageous, friendly towards people and often aggressive towards other dogs. The Akita barks infrequently and then only as a warning signal. The demeanor suggests activity and agility.

4. *Size:*

Height: Dogs 26 inches or more at the shoulder, bitches 24 inches or more at the shoulder. The male's body length to height ratio is approximately 10:9 and the female slightly greater. The dog is powerfully built, with bone and substance proportionate to height.

5. *Size and Colour:*

Double-coated. Undercoat soft and very dense and shorter than outer coat. Outer coat straight, harsh and standing somewhat off body. Hair on head, legs and ears short. Length of hair at withers and rump approximately two inches, which is slightly longer than the rest of body except tail, where coat is longest and most profuse. Any colour, brindle, white (no mask) or pinto. Colours are brilliant and clear and markings are well-balanced, with or without mask or blaze. Pinto has a white background with large, evenly-placed patches covering head and more than one-third of body. Undercoat may be a different colour from outer coat. The white Akita should have pigmented eyes, dark nose and lips.

6. *Head:*

a) Skull—massive but in balance with the body, tending to be flat on top, with the rest of the head forming a blunt triangle when viewed from top, free from excessive wrinkle when at ease, median fissure clearly visible, and stop well defined.

b) Muzzle—broad and full, distance from nose to stop is the distance from stop to occiput as two is to three.

c) Nose—broad and black, liver nose permitted on light Akitas but black always preferred.

d) Mouth—clean, powerful jaws, lips black and heavy but not pendulous, tongue pink, teeth strong with scissor bite preferred but level bite acceptable.

e) Eyes—dark brown, small, deep set and triangular in shape, eye rims black and tight.

f) Ears—the ears of the Akita are characteristic of the breed. They are strongly erect and small in relation to rest of head. If ear is folded forward for measuring length, tip will touch upper eye rim. Ears are triangular, slightly rounded at

in Show. What a plus for the bitches!

1981 . . . Our last Specialty at this writing. Held January 24, in Pomona, California, Mr. Robert Waters judged the breed; Mrs. T. Arndt, Sweepstakes.

Kuma Yama's Kazan of Koshi Ki owned by Ed and Marlene Sutton was Best Junior Sweeps Akita. Kinouk's Pudin-N-Pie of Kazan owned by N. Hemning and J. Harper was Best Senior.

Out of 169 entries in the breed competition, 39 were Specials. There were 27 absentees. Judge Waters' Best of Breed was Ch. Matsukaze's Holly go Litely, a bitch owned by B. Hunt. Best Opposite went to Ch. Satoris Asahi Go owned by Nichols and Sakayeda.

Of all the classes the Veterans had our bid for the best of the day. It is always a pleasure to see the veterans in the ring one more time. The reception given each individual was outstanding. One frequently feels these dogs should only be passed on by a breeder-judge.

1982 brought us the largest National Specialty to date: one hundred ninety-four entries, with 65 of them being Specials. There were only 37 absentees which was quite unusual for our breed. Judging was done by John Patterson and John F. Stanek. The Sweepstakes, judged by J. Hoskins, had a record entry of 82. And what a great crop of youngsters they were!

Best in Sweepstakes was a fine young bitch, Ch. Eastwind Glacier Fox of Northland. Owned and handled by Loren Egland, this typey bitch was a sterling example of the written standard for the breed in the eyes of the viewers. Small ears angled correctly over well-shaped eyes; full cheeks; tight, fully pigmented lips; correct stop and a large black nose were some of her assets.

In the regular class judging, Mr. Patterson chose his Winners Dog and Best of Winners from the Open Dog Class, Mill Creek Bozo Jo, owned by Howard and Judith Opel. The Winners Bitch, Kelly's Tara Chino, was bred and owned by Eugene and Herborg Kelly.

185

Ch. Matsukaze's Holly Go Litely, still on her winning streak from 1981, went Best of Opposite Sex.

Best of Breed, and also capturing a Working Group II the same day, was the Veteran Dog Ch. Kenjiko Royal Tenji, R.O.M. This was Jojo's 48th group placement and first Specialty win. This ten-year-old male is owned by F. Duane.

We have included pictures of this 1982 Specialty. Two American Kennel Club judges and one Akita owner-breeder judge selected these winners out of the 157 actually shown, as being those that most closely adhered to the breed standard.

What will future specialties bring forth? We are not concerned with the quantity as much as we are the quality of the entries. We are hopeful that the conscientious breeders and the concerned handlers will offer us a banquet of canine beauty for our eyes to feast upon. And, the good Lord willing, may the judges recognize these standardized beauties if they are.

BEST OF BREED
ROCHESTER, MN. K.C.
SEPT. 25, 1982
OLSON PHOTO

Ch. Eastwind Glacier Fox, Sweepstakes Winner at the 1982 National Specialty, with owner Loren Egland.   *Olson*

Mill Creek Bozo Jo CD was Winners Dog and Best of Winners at the 1982 Specialty. Sire: Krug's Yoshinori, Dam: Kirabran's Kiss-N-Tell.

Kelly's Tara Chino captured the Winners Bitch ribbon at the 1982 National. Sire: Ch. Kim-Sai's Buster of Frerose, Dam: Herborg's Hiro.

187

Best of Breed at the 1982 Akita National Specialty, Ch. Kenjikon Royal Tenji R.O.M. This veteran male has 48 group placements to his credit. Photo taken when Tenji was a youngster.

14

The Show Ring
in Japan and America

In Japan

The transition from fighting ring to show ring was accomplished by the Akita with a fair amount of ease considering the wide difference between the two.

In June, 1928, the Nipponken Hozonkai (NIPPO) was formed to aid in registering and preserving the pure Japanese breeds. The list of these breeds is extensive. There were three large-size breeds. All came from the Meiji (1868-1912) and Taisho (1912-1925) periods. They were the Takayasu Inu, the Iiyama Inu and the Akita Inur, the only one of the three which is not extinct.

In the medium-size breeds the Kai Inu, the Kishu Inu, the Hokkaido Inu and the Shikoku Inu were representatives. The small dog category had the delightful and beautiful Shiba Inu.

Nippo held its first dog show November 6, 1932 and every year following until 1942. Only native Japanese dogs were shown. Few Akitas were represented at most of these events.

Akitainu Kyokai (AKIKYO) was organized in Tokyo in October, 1948. The first Akikyo show was held the following year in conjunction with the 13th memorial services for the faithful Akita dog Hachiko.

In the beginning, it appears that it had some association

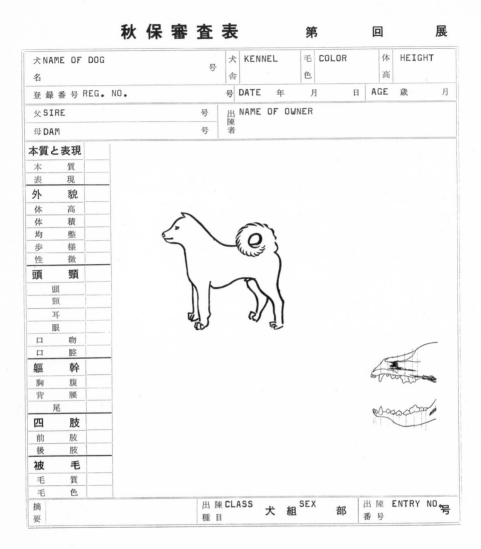

秋 保 審 査 表	第　　回　　展

犬 名 NAME OF DOG	号	犬 舎 KENNEL	毛 色 COLOR	体 高 HEIGHT

登録番号 REG. NO.	号	DATE　年　　月　　日	AGE　歳　　月

父 SIRE	号	出 陳 NAME OF OWNER
母 DAM	号	者

本質と表現	
本　　　質	
表　　　現	
外　　貌	
体　　　高	
体　　　積	
均　　　整	
歩　　　様	
性　　　徴	
頭　　頸	
頭	
頸	
耳	
眼	
口　　　吻	
口　　　腔	
軀　　幹	
胸　　　腹	
背　　　腰	
尾	
四　　肢	
前　　　肢	
後　　　肢	
被　　毛	
毛　　　質	
毛　　　色	

摘 要		出陳 種目 CLASS　犬　組 SEX　部	出陳 番号 ENTRY NO.号

Akiho individual dog judging sheet.

190

with Akiho. According to old Akiho records, Akiho recognized the establishment of the Akitainu Kyokai in Tokyo in 1949. It also shows that Mr. Katsusuke Ishihara, who was an important figure from the beginning of Akikyo, was also an Akiho judge who judged the 15th Akiho Headquarters show of 1951 and at several subsequent Headquarters shows. One is not sure for what reason Akikyo became separated from Akiho, but it seems to have occurred around April, 1955 when Akikyo became incorporated.

Since Akikyo was established rather late, after Nippo and Akiho, its main sphere of influence in the beginning was in the Kanto Region with Tokyo as the center. Later, branches were established in the Tohoku, Tokai and Tozai regions. More recently they have expanded to Chugoku, Shikoku and parts of Kyushu. However, the branches seem to be more heavily concentrated in the Kanto Region, with fewer branches scattered rather sparsely in other regions. Therefore, fewer dog shows are held by Akikyo.

The famed Akiho organization, registering body for Akitas only, held a show after World War II in November, 1947. Although shows might have been given during the war, this was considered the 11th. Sadly, records are not available.

There are three types of Akiho shows in Japan, in order, as follows:

1. Branch Shows—May have more than 300 single entries.
2. Regional Shows—Five or six branches may put on an area regional show. However, only the exceptional Branch Show winners are eligible for a Regional show.
3. Headquarters Shows—Held Spring and Fall with only the top dogs from the Regional shows allowed to enter. Entry can run upwards of 300 dogs.

All opening show ceremonies are both elaborate and solemn.

Club and Japanese colors are displayed. The National Anthem is played. Club members serve as helpers and wear colorful club jackets. Trophy tables are laden with exquisite

Sixth annual Jonan Branch Akikyo show, 9/24/55. Shiro Kuma Go Bahi is white dog in foreground.

Meiyosho winner Kumohibiki-Go. Circa 1965, in Japan.

192

Akitainu Hozonkai president, the Honorable Mr. Sasaki reading
a message prior to the Headquarters show in 1979.

Japan. Akita male with gold collars and lead.

scrolls and silver. Judges are conservatively but elegantly dressed and wear traditional red and white rosettes. Official photographers wear club armbands.

Each Japanese Akita is presented beautifully and in *full coat only*. Dogs and bitches are flawlessly groomed. They wear magnificent double collars; a round leather with a gold or silver choke chain attached. A six foot braided silk lead, in gold or red, completes the picture. Dogs and equipment are an expensive investment. Top Akitas have been sold in the $50,000 range.

There is always a head official table where persons of importance are seated. Besides the judges, officials and honored guests, government dignitaries frequently appear. Before judging, the judges are introduced. Speeches of welcome follow.

The show grounds are one huge circle inside which are several white-circled rings approximately 12 feet in diameter. Small silver bowls are placed at the edges for judges to wash hands after their "touch" examinations of each dog.

In addition to the Chief or Head Judge, there is a panel of judges whose number depends on the total entry in show. Each judge can only go over 30 individual dogs at one show. He is what we call a "Specialist judge." He judges only Akitas, has had from 10 to 20 years experience with the breed, and has apprenticed under older, more knowledgeable judges for many, many years. In most cases, he is or has been a breeder of Akitas.

The show begins with the Yoken Class, the six to ten month old dogs and bitches. Dogs are situated at one end of the ring complex, bitches at another. The judges do a written critique on each dog. Except for checking for black spots on tongue, counting teeth to ascertain correct bite and testicle check on males, they do not handle the dog. It is a visual exam. The Akitas are presented individually in a natural stance. The handlers stand well behind or to the side of their charges and are not permitted to position them. Baiting with food is not allowed.

194

Dauinke: Yoken female.

Mikasa: Seiken male.

Tochigumo: Seiken male.

Shiromi: Seiken female.

Sumitora: Soken male.

Kunihana: Soken female.

When judging of the Yoken is completed, the Wakainu or 10 to 18 month class is judged followed by the Soken or 18 to 30 month class and the Seiken or 30 month and over class.

In all of these classes the dogs are judged as to how well they adhere to the Standard, not whether one dog is better than the other.

In the afternoon, the equivalent of our American group judging is held. Placements are made from one through 15 in each class. It is conceivable to have 50 dogs in a class.

The grading system is as follows:

TOKUYU—Superior (Awarded to Senior Dogs and Bitches only)

YUSHO—Excellent

JUNYU—Good

NINTEI—Satisfactory

SHIKKAU—Disqualification (Unacceptable at that time)

The MEIYOSHO, the highest award that can be attained by an Akita in Japan, is awarded to dogs and bitches at Headquarters-sponsored shows. Only dogs and bitches who have achieved the TOKUYU rating qualify. These dogs are considered to have extra special qualities. "A Meiyosho winner," according to Mr. Zenzo Watanabe, one of the three most experienced judges of Akiho, "is not merely the top winning dog of a particular Headquarters show. As the Akita is judged according to an absolute Standard, a given show may produce a Meiyosho winner, may not produce a winner, or it may produce more than one winner. Therefore, these winners may be considered the Grand Champions of Akiho shows."

A Meiyosho winner can never compete again, only be exhibited.

Though Akiho judging procedure is different, the all-breed Japan Kennel Club shows are judged much like we do our all-breed events.

In America

All dog shows, whether all-breed or specialty, where

Hawaii's first Champion Akita, Daijoryu-Go was born in Japan on October 15, 1972. Owner is Richard Kawamoto.

Ch. Akita Tani's Yoru Bara. First female in U.S. to place in the Working Group. Owner, Mr. & Mrs. Tom Ing.

197

Ch. Tiger's Eye Storm Warning is one of the four Akitas who have gone Best in Show.

Left to right: Littermates Ch. Mitsu Kuma's Tora Oji-Go R.O.M. and Terry Wright, Ch. Mitsu Kuma's O'Kashihime and Mr. & Mrs. S. Mullen, Ch. Mitsu Kuma's Satohime-Go.

198

championship points are awarded, are held under the rules and regulations of the American Kennel Club, whose responsibility it is to approve judges, register purebred dogs and keep records of the points.

If a purebred Akita is eligible for registration with the AKC, he can compete at licensed dog shows provided he meets the qualifications of his Standard as set down by that prestigious organization, is at least six months old and does not have one of the disqualifying faults, as noted in the Standard for his breed. Lame or altered dogs should not be shown.

Before any dog steps into a show ring he should be accustomed to crowds, a leash and handling, and be well groomed. Unlike his counterpart in Japan, the Akita in America is shown with a simple choke chain and leather show lead, is often hand-stacked and baited with food.

Shows where championship points are awarded are either benched or unbenched. At a benched show, dogs must remain in partitioned stalls for all or part of the day. They are secured by a bench chain. At an unbenched show, they may be taken home after their class has been judged.

Sometimes a club holds a Sanctioned Match Show under a plan designated as "Plan 'B'" or "Plan 'A'" by AKC. No championship points are awarded at these fixtures. Many "fun matches" are given by clubs or organizations and are not sanctioned by AKC. All "matches" are important training grounds for puppies and dogs who will later compete at a "point" show.

How Dogs Are Judged

The judge is guided by the Standard of Perfection for each breed in making his selections. This standard describes what is considered a perfect specimen of the breed, and often the relative importance of each detail. The Standard also lists definite faults which are to be discouraged or penalized in the breed.

The judge must study each dog carefully, with his hands as

Ch. Ketket's Tigger no Nan Chao (Ch. Sakusaku's Uncle Louie x Ch. Sakusaku's Diamond Lil). Owners Mr. & Mrs. Henry Janicki. Bred by Anne Diener, Ketket Kennel.

The first Best in Show Akita, Ch. Wanchan's Akagumo, June, 1977. Bred and owned by Dr. and Mrs. Peter Lagus. Shown by Carol Foti.

well as his eyes; with the dog in motion as well as standing. He checks on the texture of the coat, firmness of muscle and bone, and soundness of teeth. The way a dog moves is important, not only for beauty in motion, but as a test of body structure.

There are a number of things the handler can do to show his dog to best advantage, and the dog with a lively, intelligent personality and sense of showmanship often has an advantage. But the basis of judging in the show ring is the physical beauty and structural soundness of the dog. The judge compares the dogs in each class and makes the awards to those which best meet the requirements of the standard.

Dogs get points toward a championship and qualify for the top awards as follows:

Regular Classes: All dogs competing for championship points are entered in one (or more) of the regular classes for their breed and sex. The classes are:

PUPPY: For dogs under one year. May be divided 6-9 and 9-12 months.

NOVICE: For dogs not having won three first in Novice, none in other classes, except puppy, nor any championship points.

BRED BY EXHIBITOR: For dogs not champions owned wholly or partly by breeder; shown by him or his family.

AMERICAN-BRED: For all dogs, except champions, born in the U.S.A., resulting from a mating which took place in the U.S.A.

OPEN: For any dog.

(Same classes as shown for dogs above, apply for females.)

Winners Classes:

WINNERS DOG: The first-place winner of each class for males (which has not been beaten in any other class) competes for Winners Dog. He receives a purple ribbon and points proportionate to the number of males present.

RESERVE WINNERS DOG: The second-place dog from the WD class competes with the dogs remaining in the ring, unless he has already been defeated by one of them, for

Ch. Sakusaku's Perfect Pearl. Owner Barbara Hampton. Breeder, Mr. & Mrs. G. Linderman. *Ludwig*

Ch. Chereed's Obi-Wan Kenobi (Ch. Cee-Jay's Chumley P. Linderman x Ch. Matsu-Kaze's Chereed Notakaii). Owners are Mr. & Mrs. George McKulski. Breeder, Mr. & Mrs. Reed Keffer. *Petrulis*

Reserve Winners. The RW receives a purple and white ribbon, and moves up to winners if the WD is for any reason disqualified.

WINNERS BITCH: Same procedure followed, (judging of first place winners in bitch classes) as for Winners Dog.

RESERVE WINNERS BITCH: Same procedure followed in judging as for Reserve Winners Dog.

BEST OF BREED: The Winners Dog and Winners Bitch compete with any champions entered for Best of Breed* and winners of non-regular classes such as Veteran, Local, or Field Dog (if they have not been previously defeated in a regular class), for Best of Breed. The winner receives a purple and gold ribbon.

BEST OF WINNERS: If the Winners Dog or Winners Bitch is awarded Best of Breed, it automatically is awarded Best of Breed, it automatically is awarded Best of Winners; otherwise, the Winners Dog and Winners Bitch are judged together for Best of Winners. In addition to the blue and white ribbon, the BW may receive additional points if the opposite sex had an entry qualifying for higher points.

BEST OF OPPOSITE SEX: Following selection of Best of Breed and Best of Winners all individuals of the sex opposite to BOB remain in the ring. The Winners Dog or Winners Bitch, whichever is also of the sex opposite to Best of Breed, is judged in this class. From this group, Best of Opposite Sex is chosen. A red and white ribbon is awarded to the Best of Opposite Sex to Best of Breed.

THE GROUP: The Akita belongs to the Working Group. The blue rosette for first in group is given to the winner among all Best of Breed dogs competing in that particular group. Red, yellow and white rosettes are also given to the second, third and fourth place winners in Group.

---

*Entries in the BOB class are dogs or bitches which are champions, having acquired sufficient points in previous competition. If there are no champions entered, the Best of Winners is automatically Best of Breed. The other dog or bitch competing for Best of Winners is Best of Opposite Sex.

203

BEST IN SHOW: The six Group winners are judged for the top award BEST IN SHOW. A rosette, colored red, white and blue is given.

NOTE: Four ribbons are awarded in each class—blue for first, red for second, yellow for third and white for fourth. Champions may compete in Puppy or Open classes, but are usually entered for Breed only, as they do not need the championship points awarded to Winners Dog and Winners Bitch. To become a champion, a dog or bitch must win a total of 15 points under at least three judges. Also, it must win a minimum of three points in each of two shows under different judges.

Some Closing Notes: In America, dropped tails are being seen more and more frequently. In Japan, tails are *always* well curled. When a tail is not tightly wound at all times, lack of strength and character is obvious. Uniformity of type and color abound at Japanese dog shows. As an example, in one class at one show, there were 25 reds, nine whites, eight brindles. In America, color and type are so varied, judges with limited knowledge of the breed frequently make questionable class placements. Unfortunately, few Akita breeders are licensed to judge their breed in this country. Showing an Akita in *full coat only* is a must in Japan. That is not so in America. To quote Dr. K. Ogasawara on the subject, "Would you show your pregnant wife in a beauty contest?"

Amen.

Ch. Remwood's Cub Woofie (Sakusaku's Diamond Jim x Ch. Remwood's Kuro Sumi Maru). Owners, Roger and Kathy Blase.

Ch. Ketket Dyn-O-Mite O'Sakusaku (Ch. Sakusaku's Uncle Louie x Ch. Sakusaku's Diamond Lil). Owner, J. Linderman. Handler, C. Kam.

Left to right: Ch. Cee-Jay's Portrait of Thornbrook, C.D., Ch. Cee-Jay's Climax No Noroshi. These Akitas were bred by Mr. & Mrs. J. Hoskins and are owned by C. Doernback and Gary Speed.

Pictured are Richard and Emilie Woods handling the father and daughter Ch. Tano Kita Maru To No Remwood and Ch. Remwood's Kuro Sumi Maru.

Ch. Nan Chao's Hosi no Samurai has 47 Bests of Breed to her credit. Owners: Mr. and Mrs. William Byers.

Carol Foti proudly handles her Champion bitch, Kosetsu no Sugata no Jo-San.

Ch. Oshio's Reiji, owned by Mr. and Mrs. C. Lutz.

Ch. Oshio's Maruhime-Go. Sire: Azuma Taru Maru. Dam: Miyami Norico-Go. Maru has had the distinction of winning under both Japanese and American judges.

Ch. Ketket's Elektra of Sakusaku. Bred by Anne Diener
and owned by Mr. & Mrs. G.N. Linderman.

Dr. & Mrs. Peter Lagus and Ch. Tuskos Kabuki and his sister
Tusko's Star. Bred by Mr. & Mrs. D.D. Confer.

Anita Powell's Ch. Oshio's Tami-Go.

Seven month old female, Ch. Kosetsu no Pan SuSu with owner/breeder, Carol Foti.

210

Ch. Triple K Cho Cho, C.D., owned by Mr. & Mrs. J. Hoskins.

REGISTER OF MERIT STUD DOGS

(As of February, 1982, AKC Gazette)

Akita Tani's Kuro Chikara
Akita Tani's Tatsumaki
Ch. Cee Jay's Chumley P. Linderman
Ch. Fukumoto's Ashibaya Kuma
Ch. Gaylee's O'Kaminaga
Ch. Gin-Gin's Haiyaku-Go of Sakusaku
Ch. Kenjiko Royal Tenji
Ch. Kin Ko
Mikado No Kin Hozan
Ch. Okii Yubi's Mr. Judge
Ch. Okii Yubi's Sachmo of Makoto
Ch. Sakusaku's Tom Cat-Go
Ch. Shori's Daisan Banko Maru
Ch. Taki's Akaguma Sakura
Ch. Toyo-No Charlie Brown
Ch. Triple "K" Tomo-Go
Ch. Va-Gua's Jamel The Mean Machine
Yukan No Okii Yubi

REGISTER OF MERIT BROOD BITCHES

(As of February, 1982, AKC Gazette)

Akita Tani's Kuro Shushu
Ch. Beastie of Toshiro
Ch. Butterworth Bog Sumi Mendo
Ch. Costa Brava's A Touch of Class
Ch. Don D's Dietka of the Hot
Ch. Echol's Ichi-Ban Tamiko
Ch. Fio Princess Kira of Kirabran
Frerose's Honey Bear
Ch. Frerose's Sarah Lei
Hana Hime
Hot's Kooky Kita
Ch. Jade Ko Samurai

Juho Mariko No Kin Hozan
Ch. Kimiko of Frerose
Ch. Kinouk's Kor-I
Kofuku No's Shoga Hime
Ch. Krug's Shumi Go Ditmore
Ch. Kuro Panzu Maru No Asagao
Ch. Lijo's Spirit of Tobe
Ch. Matsu-Kaze's Chereed Notakali
Ch. Matsu-Kaze's Key-Too Kinouk
Ch. Matsu-Kaze's Kuro Kitsune
Ch. Ms. Matsu-Kaze Loves Company
Ch. N Bar J's Akarri Su of Kajo
Ch. Okii Yubi's Dragonhouse Ko-Go
O'Shea Princess Bara-Go
Sakura's Chujitsu
Sakusaku's Daffodil Lil
Sakusaku Gorotsuki-Go
Ch. Sakusaku's Perfect Pearl
Shimi Kuma
Tane Matsu-Go
Ten No Tengoku
Toyo-No Namesu Joo
Ch. Triple "K" Cho Cho, C.D.

Note: The number of Champion progeny required to attain the R.O.M. (Register of Merit) award would be: 10 for dogs and 5 for bitches.

GLOSSARY

Aka: red
Mesu: female dog
Ken: prefecture
Inu: dog
Kuma: bear
Tora: tiger
Goma: sesame
Shibusa/Soboku: simplicity without adornment
Kuro: black
Buchi: pinto
Hoho-boke: faded cheek color
Shiro: white

FINIS

_____

Because some Akita fanciers in America today are drawn to the Goromaru line and others to the Kongo line, we feel it is fitting to end this treatise with a little tale about what happened when the two dogs met face to face in the show ring for the first time. Perhaps after reading this, their thoughts on which line is the better one will be satisfied.

"Goromaru having produced many famous Akitas was invited to many shows throughout Japan. One of the greatest or most satisfying moments for Goromaru came at an Akikyo show held in Tokyo. Kongo-Go was then one of the top Akitas in the country. At the above-mentioned show, both Goromaru and Kongo were invited to the show. Kongo was a silvery Goma colored dog, a sleek city prince. Goromaru was a pinto and a country product." Mr. Ichiro Ogasawara describes the meeting of the two Akitas as follows:

"The show was judged by Mr. Ryonosuke Hiraizumi and myself. We were all impressed by the two Akitas simultaneously shown at the center of the ring. Mr. Hashimoto, the handler of Kongo, threw his hat in the air several times. And each time Kongo would stand on his hind legs. On the other hand, Mr. Funakoshi, who was handling Goromaru, would advance Goromaru one step toward Kongo, then another. Both Akitas squared off, each staring each other in the eyes. Then suddenly, Kongo backed off. The match was decided."

214

BIBLIOGRAPHY

Akita Newsletter

Akita Kennel Club of America Newsletter

Akita Dog Association of America Breeders Bulletin

Akita Breeders Association Breeders Bulletin

Akita Club of America Newsletter

American Akita Breeders Akita News

The Digest of the Akita Dog Society News

Nisei Week Reports

The Aiken Journal

Insight Documents

Akita Club of Tampa Bay

The Akita — A Guide

"All About A Dog Show" — Gaines Dog Research Center

The Akita

Dog World Magazine

State of California Corporation Records

Akita Hozonkai, Los Angeles Branch

Akita Hozonkai, Japan

Private letters and papers from the collections of: Camille Kam Wong, Marge Rutherford, Linda J. Bruhn, Walter Imai, Maggie Bryant Vogl.

Mating and Whelping Akita Manual by Joan Linderman, Elizabeth Thayer and Maggie Bryant Vogl, published by the Akita Club of America.

Akiho U.S. Manual, for end of book "Finis" — Goromaru and Kongo Go, written by Susumo Fungkoshi, translated by Walter Imai, February, 1971.

BIBLIOGRAPHY

ALL OWNERS of pure-bred dogs will benefit themselves and their dogs by enriching their knowledge of breeds and of canine care, training, breeding, psychology and other important aspects of dog management. The following list of books covers further reading recommended by judges, veterinarians, breeders, trainers and other authorities. Books may be obtained at the finer book stores and pet shops, or through Howell Book House Inc., publishers, New York.

Breed Books

AFGHAN HOUND, Complete	Miller & Gilbert
AIREDALE, New Complete	Edwards
AKITA, Complete	Linderman & Funk
ALASKAN MALAMUTE, Complete	Riddle & Seeley
BASSET HOUND, Complete	Braun
BEAGLE, New Complete	Noted Authorities
BLOODHOUND, Complete	Brey & Reed
BOXER, Complete	Denlinger
BRITTANY SPANIEL, Complete	Riddle
BULLDOG, New Complete	Hanes
BULL TERRIER, New Complete	Eberhard
CAIRN TERRIER, Complete	Marvin
CHESAPEAKE BAY RETRIEVER, Complete	Cherry
CHIHUAHUA, Complete	Noted Authorities
COCKER SPANIEL, New	Kraeuchi
COLLIE, New	Official Publication of the Collie Club of America
DACHSHUND, The New	Meistrell
DALMATIAN, The	Treen
DOBERMAN PINSCHER, New	Walker
ENGLISH SETTER, New Complete	Tuck, Howell & Graef
ENGLISH SPRINGER SPANIEL, New	Goodall & Gasow
FOX TERRIER, New Complete	Silvernail
GERMAN SHEPHERD DOG, New Complete	Bennett
GERMAN SHORTHAIRED POINTER, New	Maxwell
GOLDEN RETRIEVER, New Complete	Fischer
GORDON SETTER, Complete	Look
GREAT DANE, New Complete	Noted Authorities
GREAT DANE, The—Dogdom's Apollo	Draper
GREAT PYRENEES, Complete	Strang & Giffin
IRISH SETTER, New Complete	Eldredge & Vanacore
IRISH WOLFHOUND, Complete	Starbuck
JACK RUSSEL TERRIER, Complete	Plummer
KEESHOND, Complete	Peterson
LABRADOR RETRIEVER, Complete	Warwick
LHASA APSO, Complete	Herbel
MINIATURE SCHNAUZER, Complete	Eskrigge
NEWFOUNDLAND, New Complete	Chern
NORWEGIAN ELKHOUND, New Complete	Wallo
OLD ENGLISH SHEEPDOG, Complete	Mandeville
PEKINGESE, Quigley Book of	Quigley
PEMBROKE WELSH CORGI, Complete	Sargent & Harper
POODLE, New Complete	Hopkins & Irick
POODLE CLIPPING AND GROOMING BOOK, Complete	Kalstone
ROTTWEILER, Complete	Freeman
SAMOYED, Complete	Ward
SCHIPPERKE, Official Book of	Root, Martin, Kent
SCOTTISH TERRIER, New Complete	Marvin
SHETLAND SHEEPDOG, The New	Riddle
SHIH TZU, Joy of Owning	Seranne
SHIH TZU, The (English)	Dadds
SIBERIAN HUSKY, Complete	Demidoff
TERRIERS, The Book of All	Marvin
WEST HIGHLAND WHITE TERRIER, Complete	Marvin
WHIPPET, Complete	Pegram
YORKSHIRE TERRIER, Complete	Gordon & Bennett

Breeding

ART OF BREEDING BETTER DOGS, New	Onstott
BREEDING YOUR OWN SHOW DOG	Seranne
HOW TO BREED DOGS	Whitney
HOW PUPPIES ARE BORN	Prine
INHERITANCE OF COAT COLOR IN DOGS	Little

Care and Training

COUNSELING DOG OWNERS, Evans Guide for	Evans
DOG OBEDIENCE, Complete Book of	Saunders
NOVICE, OPEN AND UTILITY COURSES	Saunders
DOG CARE AND TRAINING FOR BOYS AND GIRLS	Saunders
DOG NUTRITION, Collins Guide to	Collins
DOG TRAINING FOR KIDS	Benjamin
DOG TRAINING, Koehler Method of	Koehler
DOG TRAINING Made Easy	Tucker
GO FIND! Training Your Dog to Track	Davis
GUARD DOG TRAINING, Koehler Method of	Koehler
MOTHER KNOWS BEST—The Natural Way to Train Your Dog	Benjamin
OPEN OBEDIENCE FOR RING, HOME AND FIELD, Koehler Method of	Koehler
STONE GUIDE TO DOG GROOMING FOR ALL BREEDS	Stone
SUCCESSFUL DOG TRAINING, The Pearsall Guide to	Pearsall
TOY DOGS, Kalstone Guide to Grooming All	Kalstone
TRAINING THE RETRIEVER	Kersley
TRAINING TRACKING DOGS, Koehler Method of	Koehler
TRAINING YOUR DOG—Step by Step Manual	Volhard & Fisher
TRAINING YOUR DOG TO WIN OBEDIENCE TITLES	Morsell
TRAIN YOUR OWN GUN DOG, How to	Goodall
UTILITY DOG TRAINING, Koehler Method of	Koehler
VETERINARY HANDBOOK, Dog Owner's Home	Carlson & Giffin

General

AKC'S WORLD OF THE PURE-BRED DOG	American Kennel Club
CANINE TERMINOLOGY	Spira
COMPLETE DOG BOOK, The	Official Publication of American Kennel Club
DOG IN ACTION, The	Lyon
DOG BEHAVIOR, New Knowledge of	Pfaffenberger
DOG JUDGE'S HANDBOOK	Tietjen
DOG JUDGING, Nicholas Guide to	Nicholas
DOG PEOPLE ARE CRAZY	Riddle
DOG PSYCHOLOGY	Whitney
DOGSTEPS, Illustrated Gait at a Glance	Elliott
DOG TRICKS	Haggerty & Benjamin
ENCYCLOPEDIA OF DOGS, International	Dangerfield, Howell & Riddle
EYES THAT LEAD—Story of Guide Dogs for the Blind	Tucker
FRIEND TO FRIEND—Dogs That Help Mankind	Schwartz
FROM RICHES TO BITCHES	Shattuck
HAPPY DOG/HAPPY OWNER	Siegal
IN STITCHES OVER BITCHES	Shattuck
JUNIOR SHOWMANSHIP HANDBOOK	Brown & Mason
MY TIMES WITH DOGS	Fletcher
OUR PUPPY'S BABY BOOK (blue or pink)	
SUCCESSFUL DOG SHOWING, Forsyth Guide to	Forsyth
TRIM, GROOM & SHOW YOUR DOG, How to	Saunders
WHY DOES YOUR DOG DO THAT?	Bergman
WILD DOGS in Life and Legend	Riddle
WORLD OF SLED DOGS, From Siberia to Sport Racing	Coppinger